Peter Cloke is Deputy Head of Cullompton Comprehensive School, Devon and has taught English for fifteen years at CSE, O and A level in independent, grammar and comprehensive schools. He has been an O level and CSE examiner for the last five years. He is also the author of *Pan Study Aid Revision Cards: English Language*.

Pan Study Aids for GCSE include:

Accounts and Book-Keeping

Biology

Chemistry

Commerce

Computer Studies

Economics

English Language

French

Geography 1

Geography 2

German

History 1: World History since 1914

History 2: Britain and Europe since 1700

Human Biology

Mathematics

Physics

Sociology

Study Skills

ENGLISH LANGUAGE

Peter Cloke

A Pan Original
Pan Books   London and Sydney

First published 1987 by Pan Books Ltd,
Cavaye Place, London SW10 9PG

9 8 7 6 5 4 3 2 1

© Peter Cloke 1987

ISBN 0 330 29939 5

Text design by Peter Ward
Text illustration by M L Design
Photoset by Parker Typesetting Service, Leicester
Printed and bound in Spain by
Mateu Cromo SA, Madrid

CONTENTS

ACKNOWLEDGEMENTS

The publishers gratefully acknowledge the permission of the following examining boards for the right to reproduce specimen questions and syllabus materials for the GCSE examination:
The Northern Examining Association
The London and East Anglian Group
The Northern Ireland Schools Examination Council
The Secondary Examinations Council

INTRODUCTION TO GCSE

From 1988, there will be a single system of examining at 16 plus in England, Wales and Northern Ireland. The General Certificate of Secondary Education (GCSE) will replace the General Certificate of Education (GCE) and the Certificate of Secondary Education (CSE). In Scotland candidates will be entering for the O grade and standard grade examinations leading to the award of the Scottish Certificate of Education (SCE).

The Pan Study Aids GCSE series has been specially written by practising teachers and examiners to enable you to prepare successfully for this new examination.

GCSE introduces several important changes in the way in which you are tested. First, the examinations will be structured so that you can show *what* you know rather than what you do *not* know. Of critical importance here is the work you produce during the course of the examination year, which will be given much greater emphasis than before. Second, courses are set and marked by six examining groups instead of the previous twenty GCE/CSE boards. The groups are:

Northern Examining Association (NEA)
Midland Examining Group (MEG)
London and East Anglian Group (LEAG)
Southern Examining Group (SEG)
Welsh Joint Examinations Council (WJEC)
Northern Ireland Schools Examination Council (NISEC)

One of the most useful changes introduced by GCSE is the single award system of grades A–G. This should permit you and future employers more accurately to assess your qualifications.

GCSE	GCE O Level	CSE
A	A	–
B	B	–
C	C	1
D	D	2
E	E	3
F	F	4
G		5

Remember that, whatever examinations you take, the grades you are awarded will be based on how well you have done.

Pan Study Aids are geared for use throughout the duration of your courses. The text layout has been carefully designed to provide all the information and skills you need for GCSE and SCE examinations – please feel free to use the margins for additional notes.

NB Where questions are drawn from former O level examination papers, the following abbreviations are used to identify the boards.

UCLES	AEB
ULSEB	SUJB
O & C	SCE
JMB	SEB

GCSE ENGLISH – THE SYLLABUSES

EXAMINATION BOARD	SYLLABUS/ SCHEME No.	COURSEWORK		FINAL EXAMINATION				ORAL	NOTES
		Coursework weighting	Number of assignments	Exam weighting	Papers	Time allowed	Type of question		
Northern Examining Association (NEA)	A	50%	5	50%	1	2 hrs	Section A – response to literary test Section B – directed writing	Assessed during the course. No end-of-year test	
	B	100%	5	—	—	—	—	"	
	C	50%	5	50%	1	2 hrs	Section A – response to literary test Section B – directed writing	"	For mature students
Midland Examining Group	1	30%	4	70%	1.aural 20% 2.50%	1¼ hrs 1¾ hrs	Listening + response Continuous/ directed writing	Assessed during the course	
	2	80%	8	20%	1.aural	1¼ hrs	Listening + response	"	
	3	100%	10	—	—	—	—	"	
London and East Anglia Group	A	50%	5	50%	1	2 hrs	Understanding + response	Coursework 50% Test 50%	
	B	100%	10	—	—	—	—	Coursework 50% Test 50%	

EXAMINATION BOARD	SYLLABUS/ SCHEME No.	COURSEWORK		FINAL EXAMINATION				ORAL	NOTES
		Coursework weighting	Number of assignments	Exam weighting	Papers	Time allowed	Type of question		
The Welsh Board	A	20%	2	80%	1.50% 2.30%	2½ hrs 1½ hrs	Understanding + directed writing Expressive writing	Assessed during the course	
	B	50%	5	50%	1	2½ hrs	Understanding + directed writing	,,	
Northern Ireland Schools Examination Council	1	50%	5	50%	1 2	1¼ hrs 1¾ hrs	Comprehension Directed writing	Assessed during the course	
Southern Examining Group	A	50%	6	50%	1.25% 2.25%	1½ hrs 1½ hrs	Understanding Directed writing	Assessed during the course	
	B	100%	12	—	—	—	—	,,	
	C	20%	optional – 5 2,000 word max.	80%	1.40% 2.40%	1¾ hrs 2 hrs	Narrative + discursive Understanding + response	,,	

INTRODUCTION

This book covers all English Language syllabuses prescribed for GCSE by the six examination boards in Britain. These are listed on p.7.

Each board's examination has to comply with a set of national criteria drawn up through meetings of teachers, examination boards, the Secondary Examinations Council and the government. The aim of these criteria is to ensure that all of you who are taking the English examination are assessed consistently throughout the country and that the four main areas of Language – reading, writing, talking and listening – are examined. The GCSE in English, then, takes a wider view of what and also **how** you should be assessed.

You will find that, although there are differences in detail between what is set, each board will require you to produce COURSEWORK – written work not easily tested in timed written examinations, which you produced during your examination course – and to demonstrate your abilities in spoken language through an oral examination.

The introduction of compulsory coursework and oral assessment is the feature of the new examination which differs most from those which the GCSE replaces.

All examination boards set written papers in English and your marks for these, added to your coursework and oral assessment, make up your eventual grade in English GCSE. The assessment of your oral communication will appear as an endorsement on your certificate, using a different, shorter grade scale of numbers from 1 (highest) to 5 (lowest). Your examination in reading and writing will be graded on a seven point-scale of letters, A (highest) to G (lowest). It is important to remember that the two awards will be interdependent, so that you must achieve at least the lowest grade on **both** scales if an award is to be made. Grades will be shown on your certificates by a letter and a number (e.g. B3). An explanation of the grading system will appear on the back of the certificate.

The written papers will require you to attempt reading and writing for different purposes, for differing goals and audiences as specified in the national criteria. In the timed written examination, the emphasis will generally be on directed and practical kinds of writing, e.g. reports, letters, instructions and answering questions. In addition to these your coursework will contain pieces of descriptive, narrative and imaginative writing.

Another feature of the GCSE in English is that it is a single unified course leading to an assessment in English. Although there is a separate examination in English Literature, you must expect during your course and examination to study both literary and non-literary material.

The weighting given to the different parts of the GCSE examination in English – coursework, written papers and oral – by the different boards and within the alternative syllabuses set by some boards varies considerably. You will need to know which syllabus you are following and for which board. When you know this, you should find out exactly what type of tasks you will be expected to complete.

If you are the kind of person who works steadily but dislikes the pressure of timed examinations, then it may well be worth finding out from your examination centre whether they can offer you the opportunity to take a GCSE English *by coursework only*. Most of the boards offer this as an alternative syllabus and it may be particularly suitable for you if you have not had any practice at timed examinations for a few years.

The chapters on Coursework, Spoken English, The Essay, Other Forms of Extended Writing, Comprehension (Understanding) and Summary and Directed Writing are relevant to every syllabus. The chapter on Accuracy and Attention to Detail should be studied by all students because accuracy in these two areas is important in every part of the examination.

Each chapter contains essential information which you will need to know if you are to do yourself justice in GCSE English. You should study this information carefully and practise the skills required by working through the exercises and specimen questions from the examination boards. At the end of each chapter is a list of key points for final revision; use this to check your personal coverage of the main items in each chapter. It would also be useful to look at these main revision points immediately prior to the examination.

COURSEWORK

CONTENTS

Coursework is a selection of different pieces of writing which you complete during your examination course and submit to your teacher for assessment. The work is marked by your teacher and taken to a local meeting before it is sent away to be 'externally moderated' – that is, compared with the other candidates' work to ensure that standards of marking are the same.

The presence of a coursework component in the English and indeed *all* GCSE examinations is a very good thing, since it allows you to demonstrate a wide range of your abilities and interests under normal classroom conditions. You are not subjected to the same degree of tension and stress as you might feel in an examination which relies solely on your performance under 'formal' conditions. In the same way, coursework assessment reduces the emphasis on memory and on your ability to work quickly within a fixed time. Therefore your overall success does not stand or fall on your performance over one or two days during the examination period. In fact, a considerable amount of evidence has been gathered to show that coursework can and does provide accurate and valid assessment of your abilities in English; it may possibly reflect these more accurately than written examinations, because over time there is a balancing out of the variations in your individual performance.

Internally assessed coursework *must* account for at least 20 per cent of the marks in all the GCSE English syllabuses. Remember, however, that most examination groups will offer syllabuses which allow for assessment entirely by coursework.

The national criteria for English specify that some of your coursework should be assessed under **controlled conditions.** This means that *some* of your tasks will be given to you to be completed wholly in the classroom under your teacher's supervision. The idea here is to assess your ability to work in English right from the point where writing begins – including any drafting or editing (see Chapters 3 and 4). Note at this stage, however, that 'controlled conditions' are not the same as 'examination conditions', and that end-of-term 'tests' etc. are not acceptable.

There are different ways of assessing your coursework and you should check with your teacher at the beginning of your examination year as to which will be used. For example, you may be offered the opportunity to submit a project-type assignment for part or all of your assessment. You may also be following a syllabus in which assessment is carried out at intervals during the course, perhaps under 'controlled conditions' as mentioned above. It may be possible for any activity related to the examination which you undertake during your course of study to be assessed as it occurs and offered as a contribution to the final assessment.

It will be clear, therefore, that you will be given a wide range of choices of coursework activities and later in this chapter there will be some ideas for you to consider.

You will be offered a variety of starting points in the form of written or spoken texts and a selection of activities related to that. The examination encourages you to take responsibility for your own programme of work in selecting tasks which you feel you can tackle most competently. Chapters 3 and 4, which deal with essays and other forms of extended writing, should help you to make the most of your abilities and will offer some guidance on which kinds of writing might suit you best. Remember, though, that you will be expected to produce a *variety* of different types of work.

Your teacher will also give you an idea as to how long you should spend on each piece of coursework, as well as some guidance on how many words the piece may be. Bear in mind, however, that he or she will be unable to be too precise about how much is expected; remember too that quality is more important than quantity! Obviously different pieces will vary in length according to the purposes of the task and your interpretation of them.

When the time comes to hand in your coursework, you will need to bear these points in mind when making the selection of the required number of pieces of work:

1 Make sure that you meet the syllabus requirements in terms of different types of writing. If you are asked to include descriptive writing, reports, letters and a dialogue, ensure that these are present. (Chapter 4 will help you.)

2 Discuss the selection with your teacher. It may be worth drawing up your own list of preferred pieces and asking the teacher to do the same. You can then discuss any differences before the final selection is made.

3 You will not be allowed to copy out corrected work and submit it again, but you are allowed – and encouraged – to hand in notes and plans, scrapbooks of photos, articles etc.

4 If you have completed a project for part of your coursework, it will only be acceptable if it forms an integral part of a more extensive piece of work.

5 If you have worked in a group and that group plans to submit a completed piece of work, you will need to identify your own specific contribution.

6 Written coursework may be typed, but is usually expected to be produced on A4-size paper. You should not hand in complete exercise books, but cut out relevant pages and submit these. Each piece of work should be numbered and identified with your name, examination candidate number and centre number.

HOW YOUR TEACHER WILL PLAN YOUR COURSEWORK

There are many different ways of planning a GCSE English course, but your teacher will have borne these points in mind as your programme was being planned:

1 The need to have a balance between English Language and English Literature.
2 How these might be joined together for individual assignments over the duration of the course.
3 How the four different language modes referred to earlier – speaking, listening, reading and writing – are to be included in your work.
4 The range of material required for starting points.
5 The need to plan a course for everyone in the full ability range, i.e. to provide enough tasks in the programme to enable all students to succeed.

IDEAS FOR COURSEWORK

Your folder of work could contain:

1 Essays – of various lengths and different types (see Chapter 3, p.37).
2 Reports – as if you were writing for a newspaper or magazine (see Chapter 4, p.69).
3 Letters – of different types (see Chapter 4, p.73)
4 Interviews and conversations (see Chapter 4, p.70)
5 Dialogue and plays (see Chapter 4, p.79)
6 Diaries (see Chapter 4, p.83)
7 Summaries (see Chapter 5, p.87)
8 Diagrams and charts – e.g. plots (see Chapter 3), family tree, journey.
9 Responses to books or articles you have read (see Chapters 4, 5 and 6)
10 Projects or other personal research work.

WHAT THE EXAMINER IS LOOKING FOR

Look at Chapter 3 on Essays and Extended Writing to see how separate pieces will be marked. In general, though, your folder of work will be assessed on these criteria:

Content
Language
Structure

Your teacher will have to record your marks for each piece of work submitted, therefore you must make sure that you produce:

1 the specified number of pieces;
2 the required variety of types of writing – stories, descriptions, reports, newspaper articles etc.

Once each piece of work has been marked, your teacher will then have to award you a *coursework mark* based on the assessment of your complete folder of work.

Here is a list of points you should remember if you are to gain a high mark for your coursework:

1 Your **content** should be
   * well ordered
   * realistic
   * appropriate to the title of the piece
   * balanced
   * varied and interesting

2 Your **language** should be
   * fluent
   * appropriate to the style of writing required
   * varied, showing a broad vocabulary
   * technically correct
   * lively, with a variety of pace

3 Your **structure** should be
   * clear, with good paragraph construction
   * well organized into appropriate sentences of varied length
   * appropriate to the style of task required

KEY POINTS FOR FINAL REVISION

		YES	NO
◊	Minimum mark allocation	☐	☐
◊	Controlled conditions	☐	☐
◊	Starting points	☐	☐
◊	Handing in coursework	☐	☐
◊	Ideas for coursework	☐	☐
◊	What the examiner is looking for	☐	☐

SPOKEN ENGLISH

CONTENTS

The national criteria for English insist on a compulsory component on Oral Communication or Spoken English in the assessment and certification for GSCE. This may conjure up all sorts of horrors for you; talking in front of others can be daunting and worrying, but fluency in spoken language is very much a matter of confidence and if you read this chapter carefully you will be well on the way to gaining the understanding and confidence necessary to do well in this part of the English examination.

Remember:

1   that the part of the English examination based on reading and writing will be graded on a seven-point scale A – G and Oral Communication will be graded on a separate five-point numerical scale 1 – 5.

2   this part of the examination is compulsory if you wish to be awarded a certificate for GCSE English.

The oral component is now included for all candidates in recognition of the increased importance of spoken language. Recent studies have highlighted the very different ways in which people use spoken language. There are many skills involved and an important part of your preparation for English GCSE lies in knowing what some of these skills are and finding ways to practise them.

The national criteria state that you should perform 'a variety of tasks in a range of contexts' (Section A, para 5.1), which means that you should be ready to be assessed on your use of different kinds of spoken language in a variety of situations. In practice, this means that you should be provided with a number of language opportunities during your course; these will include everything from giving a short talk and answering questions on it to taking part in a group discussion in response to an extract from a magazine or newspaper, novel or film. Guidance on the activities you will be most likely to encounter is given at the end of this chapter.

In general terms, your examiner will be looking at your ability to vary your use of spoken language according to the demands of the audience – your teacher or your friends, for example. He will also be wanting to see if you handle 'formal' situations – giving a talk, explaining directions or describing how things work – and 'informal' situations – perhaps an interview, discussing a contribution to a group magazine – with equal ease. It is worth emphasizing that he will be concerned to see how well you listen, since speaking and listening are so closely linked.

Here is a selection of ten different specific skills in spoken language.

Pay close attention to the type of tasks which might correspond to them and practise them whenever you can.

1   *Conveying and receiving information.* Giving a talk about an interest, hobby, researched topic. Responses to questions.

2   *Narrating.* Telling a story, recounting a personal experience, summary or plan for the future.

3   *Arguing and persuading.* Giving the case for and/or against a controversial topic. Responding to questions and countering arguments.

4   *Conveying and following instructions and directions.* Describing how something works, correct/incorrect use. Responding to a pre-set task like giving directions from a road map or instruction leaflet.

5   *Describing and specifying.* Talking about a place, an event, an occurrence.

6   *Interpreting, evaluating and summarizing.* Responding to a passage of writing or statistics or a photograph.

7   *Speculating and hypothesizing.* Responding to 'What would happen if . . .?' Discussing the possible implications of a change; rules and regulations for an institution.

8   *Expressing and responding to personal feelings, opinions and attitudes.* Discussion with others of a poem, photograph or picture.

9   *Explaining.* Describing and accounting for a personal career choice; or a detailed account of a process, e.g. a recipe.

10   *Collaborating with others over a range of tasks from problem solving to planning a course of action.* Discussing with other particular ways of solving a set problem, e.g. the position of a new motorway or airport. Inevitably there is an overlap between some of these categories of skills, but in general we can think of them as being practical and tested in TWO situations – one involved in production, the *product*, and one as a *process* working.

1   Going solo – on your own – producing a *product*, e.g. a prepared talk.

2   Working with others – becoming involved in a *process*, e.g. a group discussion.

Detailed guidance in these two areas begins on p.23. With both these categories, what you say on any particular occasion and how you say it depends on a number of influences. If, for example, you feel that you are likely to be criticized by the person to whom you are talking, then you are less likely to have the confidence to do well. If you know that the particular talk you are involved in is to be assessed, then similarly you are likely to feel tense. It is important to identify the kind of talk you have been asked to do; giving a scientific account may be different from recounting the story of a day out, for example. You may be affected also by the place in which you are giving or taking part in a talk, especially if it is unfamiliar. The kind of questions you are asked during your talk may influence you too. Finally – and perhaps the most important factor of all – there is your **audience**. This could be one person or more, a familiar face or a stranger; a small group of three or four or a larger group of listeners.

Some of these factors could have a negative effect on your performance – *if you let them!* There are three strategies that will help you:

Find out, **prepare** and **practise**.

1   Find out:
    *   *when* you are being assessed.
    *   *where* you are being assessed.
    *   *how* you are being assessed.
    *   *by whom* you are being assessed.
    *   *for what purpose* you are being assessed.
    *   *what the examiner will be looking for* (see p.34).

2   *Prepare yourself:* organize materials and ideas before you start – this is especially important for set talks. Organize your thoughts before a discussion by making some notes on the topic to be debated.

3   *Practise* your talk – if possible to an audience even if it is just a tape recorder – and be aware of the need to be an active rather than passive participant in a discussion.

It is worth mentioning again that the examining boards may have different patterns of assessment for oral work. They may offer continuous or end-of-course assessment, or a combination of both.

Continuous assessment allows you to be assessed on your performance in a variety of 'oral' situations during the final year of the course. The marks you are awarded on individual tasks will be integrated at the end of the course into a single overall grade. Your teacher will have some flexibility in choosing the tasks on which he wishes to assess you. If you are working on your own, however, it is worth bearing in mind that you will generally be assessed in the two broad categories mentioned earlier – solo performance and group performance.

As with written work, continuous assessment of your oral abilities will help you particularly if you dislike end-of-year exams, so do enquire at your examination centre to see if this is part of the programme of oral work. Although more time-consuming, continuous assessment of your performance in a variety of situations is much less artificial than an end-of-course test.

If your centre only offers this end-of-course test, then you should find out what options are open to you. You could be set a discussion task of some kind, perhaps after you have given a talk, or a one-to-one interview between you and your teacher. You may find that your centre will prescribe topics for discussion or interview – find out what these are in good time before the assessment – or you might be invited to submit topics in advance. If this is the case, you may find the list on p.26 helpful.

SOLO OR INDIVIDUAL PERFORMANCE

Most examination boards have two categories for this:

1   The talk
2   The reading.

HOW TO TACKLE THE PREPARED TALK

In some ways the strategy for doing a good talk is the same as that for the written essay: choosing the right topic – one that does you justice – planning what you are going to say and thinking carefully about the beginning, the middle and the end of your talk.

You should aim to speak for at least five and probably not longer than twelve minutes. Be ready to answer questions from your audience – be it your teacher or members of a group to whom you are giving the talk. Use any visual material – pictures, photographs, diagrams or aural aids, e.g. tapes – to help you. You are unlikely to get a high grade if you merely read from a prepared sheet, but do organize your ideas into headings and brief notes to help you.

The most important task is to choose the right topic. This should be something

1   you know a great deal about;
2   in which you are really interested;
3   which you think will excite or interest your audience.

PLANNING

Once you have decided which topic fits the bill, you must choose the aspects you intend to talk about. It is helpful to display these in a diagram (see Figure 1).

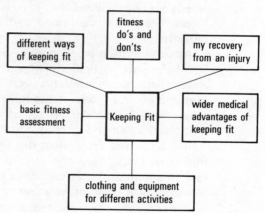

Figure 1 Spoke diagram for planning a talk.

This 'spoke' method of organizing your ideas will help you to develop your thoughts in an orderly way. However, there are other ways which you may find more useful to you – making a list of points under various headings, for example.

PLANNING EXERCISE 1

Work out your own diagrammatic plan for these topics:

Fishing
Cycling
Netball
Fashion
Going on holiday

When you have displayed your ideas in this manner, you must then decide on the sequence or order in which you are going to use them. For example:

1 Why I needed to get fit after injury.
2 Wider medical advantages of being fit.
3 Different ways of keeping fit.
4 How to assess how fit you are.
5 Do's and don'ts of keeping fit.
6 Clothing and equipment.
7 What you can expect to achieve by getting fit.

BEGINNING

If you are going to achieve a high grade, one of the things you must show is that your *structure* is good – that the way in which you have organized your ideas is clear and logical. You should introduce the subject for a minute or so, saying why you have chosen it and giving a brief outline of how you intend to introduce your discussion of it. The more interest and enthusiasm in the topic you can show, the better.

DEVELOPMENT

After the introduction, you should move to the main part of the talk – the middle or development. You should aim to spend between five and eight minutes on this (different exam boards have different requirements). This is the section which will contain the main body of ideas and information, both of which need to be developed in a clear, sensible way. In this section, you should be particularly aware of the value of using a visual aid – a picture, diagram, sketch or model which will help you to explain some of your ideas to the audience. This is important if your talk is on a mechanical or technical topic; if you can provide a model here, it will be especially valuable.

THE CONCLUSION – ENDING

One thing that will not please the examiner is if you simply stop with, 'That's about it.' Make sure you plan what you are going to say. You should allow half a minute or so for your conclusion and try to sum up your ideas without repeating what you have already said.

PLANNING EXERCISE 2

⇨ Plan a talk using a Planning Grid on one or more of these topics:
>   My hobby
>   A pop group
>   Motorbikes
>   Home brewing
>   Speedway
>   Pigeon racing
>   Changing hairstyles
>   Horses
>   Pets
>   Model engineering
>   Blood sports
>   Nuclear power
>   Snooker

GIVING YOUR TALK – DO'S AND DON'TS

If you have prepared your talk carefully and thoroughly, you are well on the way to getting a good grade in the oral examination. A lively, sound and interesting presentation is most important. These points will help:

1 **Speak clearly**, taking care that everyone can hear you. However, bear in mind your audience; if it's a one-to-one talk, don't start off as if you are giving a lecture in a hall!

2 **Be enthusiastic**, show that you are **interested** – especially at the beginning of your talk. You need to gain the attention of your audience and maintain their interest in what you have to say.

3 Be positive and friendly; look at your audience – eye contact is important.

4 Be ready to pause after making an important point – allow what you have said to sink in! Be prepared to respond to any questions as you go along, especially if your talk is on a technological or scientific topic.

5 By all means refer to your notes on the postcard, but **don't try to learn your talk off by heart**. This is the road to disaster! Not only will the examiner have been instructed by the examination board to allow fewer marks if you recite your talk or repeat it parrot fashion, but also your talk will sound boring and dull. In addition, there is also a real danger of your losing the track of your delivery if you are interrupted by a question from the audience.

6 If you are using pictures or other materials to show the audience, decide *how* you are going to use them. If you choose to pass them round, be sure that you do not rush ahead with the rest of your talk while the audience is still examining one of your visual aids.

7   Be ready to **respond to questions** at the end of your talk. Adopt a positive approach here and invite questions from the audience. You will find two general areas of interest.

  *   Questions asking for a **personal response** – such as 'Why have you chosen this topic?' or 'What advice would you give to someone who would like to take up (stamp collecting, cycling, etc.)?'

  *   Questions which ask you to go into more **explanatory detail** on something you have said, e.g. 'Why do you have to adjust your handlebars at the same time as the seat?'

Dealing with such questions is an important part of your talk. Remember that if you have prepared thoroughly you will have the knowledge and information to hand, so listen and think carefully before you answer, then speak up clearly and confidently. Above all, value the question and be seen to take it seriously.

Finally, keep a sense of humour, be positive and friendly; try not to be too intense and withdrawn – be approachable!

THE READING

You may be assessed in one of two ways:

1   You will be asked to read a prepared passage of about 500 words from a book, newspaper or magazine of your choice. You introduce the extract or article and answer questions after the reading.

2   You are given an extract from a novel, play or poem you know and after introducing the reading you are asked questions on it. Some examination boards may give you the specific extract well in advance of the test. Others may allow you just a few minutes' preparation time beforehand.

HOW TO TACKLE THE PREPARED READING

Don't choose the reading task as a soft option for your oral assessment. It isn't! It may seem to require much less hard work than preparing a talk, but it does in fact demand a most thorough preparation, skilful presentation and the thoughtful answering of questions.

No matter if you or your teacher have selected the passage from the chosen book or play etc., remember these points:

1   You should have read the whole text beforehand.

2   Make sure you understand the link between your reading passage and the rest of the plot and the roles played by characters.

3   Choose a passage which is important in that it tells the audience something interesting and essential to the development of the plot or characters.

4   Aim for a passage which has both speaking (dialogue) and story telling (narrative); this will help you to show the range of your reading skills.

5   Make sure that you time yourself before the test – if this is possible –

to ensure that your passage is long enough to meet the demands of the examination board.

6 If *you* have chosen the passage, jot down the reasons why. You will most certainly be asked this when you have finished reading.

Another important part of the preparation lies in asking yourself a few key questions:

* Where shall I pause?
* Where do I need to read more quickly or more slowly?
* Are there any difficult words or expressions which I need to practise?

Using a cassette recorder, try practising the reading beforehand and act as your own critic. Ask yourself if your reading is interesting and lively and in keeping with the rest of the text. If you are practising a dialogue, have you varied your voice for different characters?

PRESENTING THE READING

1 Start off with an introduction:
* Title and author of the text from which your passage is taken.
* A very brief outline of the plot in a few sentences.
* Set the scene, identifying the link between your passage and the plot.
2 Remember to speak clearly and to look up from time to time – involve the audience in your reading.
3 Vary pitch, pace, tone and emphasis fully so as to bring out differences between characters or dramatic incidents in your passage. Remember that the more dramatically you use your voice, the greater the display of your reading skills.
4 Enjoy the reading – be enthusiastic.

OTHER TYPES OF SOLO PERFORMANCE

Possibly your examination board provides opportunities – usually as part of oral coursework – to carry out some other types of activity, such as:

1 Introducing a topic for group discussion.
2 Reporting back on the discussion.
3 Preparing a motion in a debate (see p.31).

Follow the guidelines for preparation of the solo performance for talks if you have the opportunity to carry out tasks like these.

GROUP PERFORMANCE

Your examination board will almost certainly have part of its assessment devoted to group performance – activities which involve you in talking with up to three or four others. This could involve you in:

1 A discussion of a prepared subject by a small group of others.
2 Debates.

3   Improvised or scripted drama and role play.
4   Conversations with one or more persons on various subjects or in various situations.

DISCUSSION

A discussion offers you the opportunity to demonstrate your oral skills in situations where collaboration and co-operation with others are really important. It is basically a friendly exchange of views on your chosen topic. There are three main skills involved, testing your ability to:
*   put forward, defend and/or adapt your point of view;
*   assess what has been said;
*   listen to the ideas of others.

The great danger in discussion is that you may interrupt without thinking and offer dismissive or unconstructive comments. These are dangers to be avoided at all costs.

By all means be ready to contribute, but base what you say on your own experiences or knowledge.

Of central importance to your discussion will be the choice of topic. These are in two general areas:
*   Responding to a question based on a group reading of a piece of prose, a poem, magazine or newspaper extract or viewing of a TV programme *or*
*   Discussing a controversial topic such as blood sports, capital punishment etc.

Note these points:

1   It is usually better to have a question to answer on a selected topic. For example: *Topic*: Violence on television. *Question*: 'How far do you think the rise in crimes of violence is due to the amount of violence on television?'
2   If your teacher asks you to make the choice, you may find the list of controversial topics on p.31 helpful.
3   Try to limit your discussion – avoid getting involved on too broad a front.

Before you begin your discussion, you should work individually to list the main points and issues you feel are important. Your examiner will be looking to see if you have something to offer, so be ready to show him that you have. Your individual work and research are most important, so don't underestimate the time this can take. If you are discussing the link between the wearing of seat-belts and the number of road accidents, for example, obtain the most recent statistics and be ready to use them in your contribution.

BEGINNING THE DISCUSSION

Note these points:

1   Sit where you can see everyone in the group, possibly in an arc.
2   One member of the group will have to start, one may possibly have to

report back following a summing up. Decide who is to take on these roles if the examiner requires them.

3   It is a good idea for all members of the group to make an initial statement on the issue to be discussed. Use your notes and research to help you here; try to use *facts* to precede and support *opinion*.

DEVELOPING THE DISCUSSION

4   Think carefully about others' contributions. Remember that the examiner will be looking to see how well you **LISTEN**. Jot down brief notes to help you.

5   The discussion should arise naturally from your response to what the other members of the group have said. There may well be conflicting views and the examiner will be looking for your ability to listen to them sympathetically and to change the direction of the discussion if necessary.

6   Remember that this is a *group* discussion and credit will be given for your awareness of the need to introduce and encourage the more reluctant members of the group.

SUMMING UP

You may have been given a time limit. If this is the case, note:

1   You might give a concluding statement, offering a balanced reflection on your own view in the light of the discussion.

2   You don't necessarily *have to* conclude. If the discussion has become lively and on-going, so much the better. A discussion cannot be as definitely organized as a set talk, reading or piece of extended writing.

WHAT THE EXAMINER WILL BE LOOKING FOR

Marks are awarded for:

1   Organization of ideas.
2   Clarity of diction, appropriate pace, volume and inflection.
3   Directness of communication, including the ability to involve the listener.
4   Giving convincing expression to thoughts and feelings.
5   Developing, illustrating and explaining ideas, opinions and feelings.
6   Responding to changes in the direction of the conversation/discussion.
7   Reacting intelligently to new ideas, and modifying or defending a position as appropriate.

Group discussion should furnish evidence of the following characteristics:

1   An understanding of the topic or themes under discussion.
2   The intelligence and relevance of observation and argument.
3   The ability to change the direction of a discussion.
4   The capacity to lead as well as listen.

5 The capacity for clear and logical thinking.
6 The maturity of style, vocabulary and phrasing and the degree of tact and sensitivity in the use of language.

CONTROVERSIAL TOPICS – IDEAS FOR DISCUSSION

Racial discrimination
Capital punishment
School uniform
The monarchy
Apartheid
Blood sports
Banning smoking in public places

Nuclear power
Press and TV censorship
Drugs in society
Compulsory wearing of crash
    helmets for motorcyclists
Tobacco sponsorship in sport
Compulsory schooling

▶ **PLANNING EXERCISE**

↷ Copy out the grid below and practise your preparation for a discussion on some of the topics above.

Topic title ....
My opening view ....

Supporting facts	Supporting opinions	Other views

My concluding view ....

DEBATES

A debate is really an organized discussion in which you argue from opposing viewpoints. It differs from a group discussion in that there are usually two teams – often of three or four members each – which put forward their views as clearly and enthusiastically as possible in order to win a vote from the audience. It is a much more formal process than a discussion, with speakers having a definite time and place to speak. Some of the terms associated with debates are:

* The Motion – the subject to be debated.
* The Proposers – those who speak *for* the topic.
* The Opposers – those who speak *against* the topic.
* The House – the audience.
* The Chairman – the person responsible for introducing the motion, for organizing the structure of the debate.

If you are one of the speakers in a debate, you must **prepare yourself** very thoroughly. Remember that you will be performing in front of an audience, which is likely to be critical and responsive. You must decide (*a*) who is to present which arguments and (*b*) the best order for presenting them. You and your partner should also consider what the opposition is likely to argue, and be ready to respond to their points; have a notepad available so that you can speak from an informed position. Also remember that you can expect some questions from the audience.

Unlike the group discussion, in a debate you will be expected to refute whatever points the opposition makes against you, and to stick to your guns.

The usual order of speaking is as follows. Note that the chairman introduces each speaker, often formally thanking the previous speaker.

1   Chairman introduces the motion and the proposers and opposers.
2   First proposer speaks in support of the motion.
3   First opposer speaks against the motion.
4   Second proposer speaks   ⎫   usually supporting first speaker
5   Second opposer speaks   ⎬   and refuting opposition's views.
6   Questions from the audience.
7   Summing up by one of the proposers.
8   Summing up by one of the opposers.
9   Vote: those in favour or against (Chairman may use a casting vote).
10   Motion declared 'carried' or 'defeated'.

WHAT THE EXAMINER WILL BE LOOKING FOR

Marks will be awarded for:
1   Quality of preparation.
2   Understanding of the subject.
3   Clarity and fluency of speech.
4   Ability to argue sensibly and convincingly.
5   Ability to listen to opponents' views and to argue against them.

SCRIPTED OR IMPROVISED DRAMA AND ROLE PLAY

SCRIPTED DRAMA

Scripted drama is based on a text for you to follow, so if this is one of the activities you are offered re-read the section on solo reading. It becomes a group activity, however, when you have to show responsiveness to the moods, feelings, ideas and promptings of other characters. Remember, though, that you are *not* being assessed in your ability to act, so your examiner will not be concerned with how effectively you move, gesture or use costume.

Bear in mind that if you are to be assessed on your use of language in scripted drama, your speaking part must be sufficiently large to enable you to demonstrate the oral skills which are being evaluated. This point also applies to activities in the next section.

IMPROVISED DRAMA AND ROLE PLAY

Improvised drama and role play are challenging activities in which you are generally presented with a situation and asked to assume the role of a person within it. You can prepare for the situation, but you cannot predict the way in which the dialogue will develop. Preparation takes the form of discussion with your partner or group and the development involves a strong degree of spontaneity in how you respond to other people's conversations. Practice is the key to successful improvised work and role play. To take on this type of task without adequate practice and preparation is not advised; you are most unlikely to do yourself justice.

WHAT THE EXAMINER WILL BE LOOKING FOR

In addition to the criteria for solo reading, you will be assessed on your ability to:

1 understand your role and interpret, sustain and present it in appropriate ways and forms of language such as discussion, argument etc.;
2 speak audibly and convincingly;
3 respond sensitively to the language and conversation initiated by other members of the group.

IMPROVISED DRAMA AND ROLE PLAY – SITUATIONS FOR PRACTICE

1 The doctor's waiting room.
2 Stuck in the lift.
3 The interview.
4 A row with the neighbours.
5 The night I arrived home late again.
6 In the queue at the supermarket.
7 A mistake at the hairdresser's.
8 There was a knock at the door . . .
9 As I went in, the room went quiet.
10 I hadn't meant to miss the train.

CONVERSATION

A conversation is an informal exchange of views and ideas. It is less structured than a discussion and more natural than an improvisation or role play, though it can have some of their characteristics. A telephone conversation, for example, in which you apologise to a friend for having lost a record/football/etc., for having broken a borrowed cycle or torn a borrowed dress, could involve a full range of language opportunities. You might like to practise the following *conversation starter* questions with a friend. (N.B. These activities will build up your confidence in oral language even if you are not assessed on 'conversation'.)

1 Did you hear about .... ?
2 Have you seen your report .... ?
3 Where are you going on holiday .... ?
4 Have you seen Richard's new kite... ?
5 Hello, is that the travel agent .... ?
6 Who would have guessed that .... ?
7 Hello, aren't you in school today .... ?
8 Did you hear what happened to John in the snow?
9 Have you come home on your own?
10 I'll never speak to her again. Will *you*?

ASSESSMENT OF SPOKEN ENGLISH

You have already been given some idea of what the examiners will be looking for. It is the purpose of this final section to see how they organize their assessment of your spoken English.

Here is a list of points to remember if you are to gain a high mark in this part of the GCSE examination.

You should use:

1 Clear speech, appropriate tone and pace.
2 A range of speech styles according to situation and audience.

You should show the ability to:

1 Convey straightforward and complex information.
2 Evaluate spoken and written material and decide what is relevant for specific purposes.
3 Describe and reflect upon experience.
4 Recognize opinions and attitudes and identify the assumptions underlying them.
5 Order and present facts, opinions and ideas with clarity and accuracy.

For your spoken English during the year, your progress will be recorded on an *assessment record sheet*. This might look like Figure 2.

EXAMINING GROUP NAME

Centre Name ....Centre Number ....Candidate Name ....

No	Date	Description of task	Situation – individual – group	Notes
1	10 Oct 1987	Prepared talk on 'Cycling'	Group	Good diagram

_____ _____ _____ _____ _____

_____ _____ _____ _____ _____

_____ _____ _____ _____ _____

_____ _____ _____ _____ _____

_____ _____ _____ _____ _____

_____ _____ _____ _____ _____

_____ _____ _____ _____ _____

Figure 2 Assessment record sheet

IDEAS FOR SELF-ASSESSMENT

TALKS
1 Use a tape recorder to record your talk.
2 Exchange tapes with a friend and comment on each other's talks.

GROUP PERFORMANCE

Use a tape recorder or video recorder to:
* look at each person's contribution;
* examine the range of skills exhibited by each person;
* check that the group kept 'on task' and did not wander too far off the topic;
* check that the object of the discussion was achieved and that there was evidence of a beginning, a middle and an end.

The point of these exercises is to encourage you
(a)　to **be self-critical**;
(b)　to build up your talk and performance in the light of what the examiner will be looking for.

Spoken English is an important part of the GCSE in English. There is absolutely no reason why you should not do well if you follow the advice given in this chapter. Remember:

1 **find out**
2 **prepare**
3 **practise.**

KEY POINTS FOR FINAL REVISION

	YES	NO
Grades	☐	☐
Ten skills and types of tasks	☐	☐
Process and product	☐	☐
Find out (six points)	☐	☐
Prepare and practise	☐	☐
Oral work – continuous assessment	☐	☐
Individual performance	☐	☐
(a) prepared talk — do's and don'ts	☐	☐
— planning exercises	☐	☐
(b) reading — presentation	☐	☐
Group performance	☐	☐
(a) discussion — what the examiner will be looking for	☐	☐
— ideas for discussion	☐	☐
— planning exercises	☐	☐
(b) debate	☐	☐
(c) scripted or improvised drama or role play	☐	☐
(d) conversation	☐	☐
Ideas for self-assessment	☐	☐

THE ESSAY

CONTENTS

The Essay is of **central importance** in the GCSE English examination. You will be required to write essays or other pieces of continuous writing for your coursework and for any end-of-course examination. The GCSE differs from previous examinations you may be familiar with in that you will be rarely given definitive guidelines such as 'Write between 450 and 500 words on one of the following titles'. Instead, your examiner will give you credit for **rough drafts**, for **notes** and **plans** which are an important part of any writer's work. The kinds of essays you produce will have to be of different types too; each examination board will specify a number of pieces of work to be submitted in your coursework folder. For example, an examination board might require for coursework:

> Five pieces of work of an approximate total length of 2,500 words. A variety of writing is required and at least two of the pieces must be written in response to literature read during the course. The six pieces should include at least one of each of the following types of writing
> > descriptive
> > narrative
> > creative.

The main idea of essay writing is for the examiner to test your writing ability through scrutiny of the organization and expression of your ideas. You will find more details of what the examiners are looking for at the end of this chapter.

Chapter 4 deals with the different types of writing you may be asked to produce; in this chapter we shall look at the different types of essay to enable you to realize what type of writing is required of you.

We can classify essays in a general sense into five categories:

1 Narrative essays.
2 Descriptive essays.
3 Discursive/argumentative essays.
4 Personal/reflective essays.
5 Factual essays.

For each of these categories, two things are of common importance:

* planning
* structure.

If you can get these two right, you are well on the way to success.

PLANNING

It is fatal to start the actual writing of your piece without adequately planning it first. No professional writer would try to write without any preliminary plan, so only a foolish amateur would imagine he has the ability to do without one. Remember that in GCSE planning is recognized as an activity to be assessed, so careful attention to this part of your work can only gain you marks. Remember also that any drafts, notes of plans etc. must be handed in with the completed work if you are to receive any credit for your planning.

Usually, your ideas on a chosen topic will spring to mind in a very haphazard way when you begin to think about it. It is important that you jot down these ideas in note form first, as they occur to you. Once all your ideas have been written down in this way, then you can begin to assemble them in a more logical order; this will provide you with material for a number of separate paragraphs.

METHOD 1

There are a number of ways of getting your ideas down on paper at this early stage. You could list them as they came to mind, e.g. *Title – My Childhood*.

> early memories – my house – my room – my parents – relatives – first day at school – friends and neighbours – special events – places I remember.

Here is an example:

Title: Christmas Day

1 Day at home with family – attitudes of mother, father, etc.
2 Christmas dinner – turkey, Christmas pudding, mince pies, wine.
3 Church service – packed church, topical sermon.
4 Presents – giving and receiving, coloured wrappings.
5 Visits from friends and relatives – more presents, noise.
6 Queen's Speech – keep quiet for a few minutes.
7 Christmas Day in days gone by – workhouse, Dickens' Christmas.
8 Decorations – cards, streamers, tree.
9 Unhappy people at Christmas – being alone or far from home.
10 Clearing up – washing up, tidying up.
11 Children waking up early – finding presents.
12 Showing off presents to visitors and friends.
13 Going away for Christmas – not as nice as Christmas at home.
14 Pantomime visits – better than TV.
15 Having a walk – getting some fresh air.

By separating these various ideas and placing them under a number of separate headings, a pattern emerges of an essay which contains five main paragraphs.

1 Christmas Day for the family at home.
2 Christmas Day visits from friends and relatives.
3 Christmas Day eating and drinking.

4   Christmas Day and its various activities and entertainments.
5   Christmas Day for less fortunate people.
     With the addition of an introduction and a conclusion, this could be developed into an acceptable essay.

METHOD 2

You might find that a diagram or planning 'web' helps you to list your ideas more clearly. The idea here is to write down the title of the work in the centre of a diagram and then list the points you wish to include – think of a cycle wheel and spokes radiating out from the centre. Look at this second way of organizing the same material for 'My Childhood'.

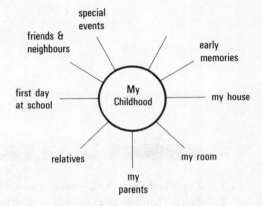

Figure 3 Web or spoke method of essay planning.

One of the advantages of this method is that you can subsequently develop ideas on each of the spokes (see Figure 4).

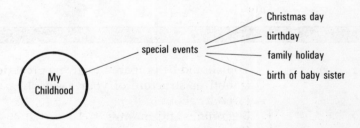

Figure 4 Developing ideas.

So not only does this diagram help to give you a number of paragraphs; it also gives you the content of these paragraphs and ensures that you do not lose the line of thought as you develop your essay.

Remember that the idea of planning your essay is to give you the structure – especially the paragraphs – in the finished product. So your next important task is to decide on the order of your paragraphs.

A simple way to do this would be to number the spokes as in Figure 5.

Figure 5 Numbering paragraphs.

▶ **PLANNING EXERCISE**

1 Organize the notes for Christmas day on p.40, into a planning web.
2 Prepare notes on diagrammatic webs for these titles:
* Holiday abroad.
* A fishing trip.
* Fashion.
Note that there will be more worked examples of essay plans later in this chapter.

STRUCTURE

You should be prepared to give a great deal of thought to the organization or structure of your essay. In particular you need to think carefully about:

1 Beginnings and endings.
2 Paragraphs.

BEGINNINGS AND ENDINGS

The examiner will look to see how effectively you introduce and conclude your essay; from these two paragraphs his overall impression of your work is helped to be formed, so it is worth taking a little extra time over them.

With your opening sentences you must arrest the interest of your examiner at once and make him want to read on. An excellent idea is to write a four- or five-word sentence. A dull opening will tend to discourage him and make it much more difficult to impress him with the rest of your essay.

♦ **'BEGINNINGS' EXERCISE**

▷ Write four- or five-word starter sentences for each of these titles:
1 The Fog.
2 Parenthood.
3 Pets.
4 The new neighbours.
5 Street accident.

There are a number of different methods you can adopt when you begin your essay depending on the type of essay you intend to write. The narrative essay could begin with a sudden startling revelation, capturing the examiner's attention at once. The argumentative essay could begin with a short anecdote, or perhaps a proverb, illustrating the stance you are about to take or the issue you are about to discuss. The descriptive essay might begin with an apt quotation, as could the reflective essay.

Examiners often criticize essays which begin with the same dull or far-fetched formula: 'It is Monday, February 24th, and I am John Smith, captain of the Spaceship *Superstar*.' Candidates are also often criticized for writing factual essays which begin with 'There are many kinds of . . .' followed by a list. Compare the effect of beginning an essay on 'Mountains' by:

> There are many different kinds of mountains; big ones and small ones, steep ones and sloping ones, cold ones and hot ones.,

with

> I shall never climb another mountain as long as I live.

The second example is much more direct, therefore much more likely to arouse the examiner's interest and make him wonder why you have come to this particular decision. He will want to read on in order to find out.

The closing paragraph of your essay is equally important, since it will provide the final impression that the examiner will have of your work. You must avoid:
1 Feebleness.
2 Dullness.
3 Assumptions.
Many good essays have been spoilt because they trail off into dull

insignificance as the writer seems to run out of inspiration and concludes with a few weak, meaningless words. You must also avoid ending so abruptly that the reader is left wondering what has happened. Examiners complain from time to time that essays have been ended as if candidates had been suddenly shot dead before they had time to complete their work! Avoid both of these extremes when you come to write a conclusion to your essay.

Various endings suggest themselves as being suitable for particular types of essay. The argumentative essay is probably best concluded by a short summary of the main points already made, or else with a final, telling point that you feel will clinch your argument. A surprise ending in the narrative essay is always something to aim for if you can. The descriptive essay could end effectively with some general impression of various details already described in the body of the essay. A final look into the future is a suitable way of concluding a reflective essay. This particular method can be used as an ending to many kinds of work, especially if it is done in a thoughtful rather than an incredible manner.

The important thing to remember is that your conclusion must be positive. It must be quite clear to the examiner that you have said all you want to say and that a definite ending has been reached.

◆ PLANNING EXERCISE

⇨ *Design* diagrammatic web plans for the titles.
⇨ *Write* introductions and concluding paragraphs for them.
1 The Risk
2 Never again.
3 Downstream Journey.
4 The fairground.
5 Winter in the countryside.
6 Nuclear weapons on British soil.
7 Footsteps in the snow.
8 The scrapyard.
9 A person I'll never forget.
10 Street fire.

PARAGRAPHS

You will stand to gain or lose a lot of marks for your structuring skills. This means that the examiner will be looking at:
1 Your overall plan.
2 Your paragraphs.
3 Your sentences within the paragraphs.
A paragraph is a collection of sentences on a particular theme. When you change the theme you change the paragraph. A good essay will be characterized, amongst other things, by evidence of control over ideas and expression through the use of paragraphs.

Here are some of the most common faults noted by examiners concerning the use/misuse of paragraphs.

PARAGRAPHS – COMMON FAULTS

1 The whole essay is written in one huge paragraph.
2 The writing is organized into dozens of tiny paragraphs.
3 Lines are missed between paragraphs.
4 There is no consistent pattern of layout. Some paragraphs begin below the last word of the last sentence, while others begin at, or are inset from, the margin.

PARAGRAPHS – POINTS TO REMEMBER

1 The way of planning your work outlined earlier in this chapter should give you the detailed method of expressing your ideas in paragraphs.
2 If your writing is characterized by one or more of the faults listed above, do spend time listing and organizing your ideas prior to writing.
3 A good essay will contain:
   * A limited number of paragraphs – perhaps six or seven.
   * Paragraphs of variable but reasonable length.
   * Paragraphs, each one of which consists of material about one topic.
4 Begin each paragraph on the line below the last line of writing, with your first word about one inch from the left margin.

PARAGRAPHING EXERCISES

◊ Write single paragraphs on each of these ideas:
1 The silliest school rule.
2 My ideal birthday present.
3 One cause of vandalism.
3 A memorable face.
3 Sunset.

Remember, then, that careful and thorough planning plus evidence of good paragraphing skills will stand you in good stead for obtaining a high mark.

You may be concerned about how long you should allow for planning. Remember that your examiner will look at your *plans and notes as part of his assessment of your work*, so it is important not to rush. As a rough idea, you should allow ten or fifteen minutes of written planning for every forty-five minutes of continuous writing. This is only an approximate guide, however, and the nature of the task will dictate different allowances of time.

THE NARRATIVE ESSAY

A narrative either describes a series of actions or tells a story. Narrative essays such as 'The Cave' or 'Midnight Adventure' always look attractive, because everyone feels it is easy to tell a story. All the examination boards insist upon at least one narrative essay being included in the coursework folder, although you are less certain of finding opportunities to write extended narratives in any end-of-course examination.

PITFALLS

There are a number of things you must NOT do if you are to achieve a good grade for a narrative essay.

1 Do *not* retell the story of a film you may have seen on TV or the cinema. You will not be able to condense the story into an apparently original plot and your examiner may already have seen the film!
2 Avoid telling a story of crime and violence, of pirates and smugglers, which usually ends up with the hero beating the villain.
3 Do *not* tell a story about ghosts, vampires or monsters, as these usually culminate in a variety of totally unreal and unbelievable situations.
4 At the end of your story, do not suddenly pretend that the whole thing has been a dream and 'then I woke up'. This is a common fault and you should avoid it if you possibly can.
5 Do not use slang expressions, even when attempting to reproduce realistic dialogue.

GUIDELINES

PLOT

1 Stick to a previously written *plan*.
2 Keep the plot simple.
3 Stick to the title – don't let your writing drift away from its planned direction.
4 Remember that the easiest way to handle narrative is a series of events in order; beginning, middle and end.

BEGINNING

Beginning a narrative is often the most difficult part. You may have thought out your plot via a diagrammatic plan, but getting started is difficult. First of all, remember what has already been said earlier in this chapter, about beginnings, then try these ways in:

1 Offer a dramatic, unusual detail, e.g. 'The piercing rain hammered the tin roof.'
2 Go straight into your action, e.g. 'The ambulance raced to the scene, sirens howling.'

3   Set the scene of the story (but don't go on too long!), e.g. 'We had endured each other's company for six long weeks. Now it was back to Idesholt Comprehensive School for a promising term.'

4   Use dramatic dialogue, e.g. 'Get off now', he growled. 'This is the end of the line for you.'

THE MIDDLE – OR DEVELOPMENT

It is important here to:

1   Involve a reasonable amount of credible action which is linked together into a logical order.

2   Link your development with your introduction.

3   Use good **descriptive detail** about characters, places and events.

4   Pay particular attention to your plan so as to ensure that there are no gaps in your development.

5   Stick to the **same tense**. Do not jump about from the past to the present. If in doubt, then stick to the past tense for your story and you will not become confused.

THE ENDING

Remember:

1   Read what has already been written in this chapter about endings.

2   Round off your story.

3   Avoid leaving the ending in mid-air. This is a strategy which can be very effective when done satisfactorily, but it is risky to attempt unless you are practised.

4   Think about an unexpected ending. This is best planned from the outset via a technique which involves you in deciding what 'twist' you are going to introduce at the end of your story, and then working backwards from this.

CHARACTERS

Try to paint a word picture of your characters. The more they can be described in detail and the more they contrast with each other, the better.

   The description of characters is best done by paying close attention to:

1   Their physical appearance – especially facial detail and expression – and dress.

2   Their apparent personalities – outgoing/withdrawn/happy/moody etc.

3   What they say and how they say it.

4   What they do and how they do it.

◆ **CHARACTER PLANNING – EXERCISE**

◇ Invent four characters who will form the basis for these stories. Use the grid (see Figure 6) for character planning if this helps.

1 The hijack
2 The end of the road
3 Time stood still
4 The zoo visit
5 The dare

Figure 6 Character planning grid

TITLE OF STORY:

Character's name	Age	Face	Physical features	Dress	Personality	Speech	Actions

Example of a Narrative Essay Plan

The title is 'Lost in the Fog', and the planning web is shown in Figure 7.

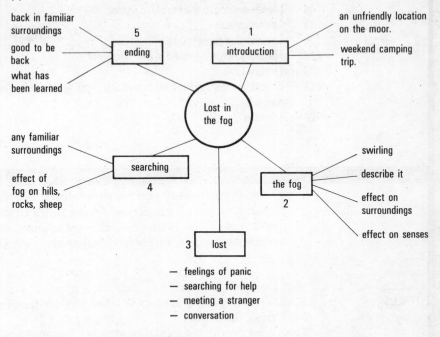

back in familiar
surroundings

good to be
back

what has
been learned

5 ending

1 introduction

an unfriendly location
on the moor.

weekend camping
trip.

Lost in
the fog

any familiar
surroundings

effect of
fog on hills,
rocks, sheep

searching
4

the fog
2

swirling

describe it

effect on
surroundings

effect on senses

3 lost

— feelings of panic
— searching for help
— meeting a stranger
— conversation

Figure 7 Planning web for 'Lost in the fog'.

NARRATIVE ASSIGNMENTS

◇ Use these introductions as starting points for plans – or full narration of your own.

1 'I know just how he felt.' Tell a story which at some point includes these words.
2 'Never again,' I said. Write a story which leads up to you making this comment.
3 Use these ingredients to invent a story with an unexpected ending:
   *   a tramp; motorway service station; a helicopter; thunderstorm.
   *   a lorry driver; a swimming pool; a rusty knife; a sandstorm.
   *   a schoolteacher; a sledge; strong wind, ice-cream van.
4 Write your own version of the 'Good Samaritan' story.
5 There could be no turning back.
6 The risk.
7 Write an essay beginning or ending with one of these sentences:
   *   I saw it, last Saturday, at the house near the end of the road.
   *   Who would have guessed that a day which started so badly would have turned out so well?
   *   I knew I shouldn't have gone to that fortune teller.
8 A day out I'll never forget.
9 A knock at the door was heard above the howling wind.
10 A leap in the dark.

11   Locked out.
12   Caught red-handed.
13   A blessing in disguise.
14   I never wanted to see the place again.
15   The hostage.
16   The warning came too late.
17   The shadows lengthened in the moonlight.
18   The last time.
19   Write a story suggested by one of the pictures you have seen in a recent newspaper or magazine.
20   The attic.

THE DESCRIPTIVE ESSAY

In this type of essay you normally describe people, scenes or events. Remember that a good description relies upon **careful observation** and to get a good mark you will need to show an eye for detail, a wide vocabulary and an ability to visualize and describe accurately.

PITFALLS

1   Do not wander off the topic – keep to the description.
2   Do not tell a story.
3   Avoid producing a catalogue of the features you are describing.
4   Be wary of describing something you know nothing about.

GUIDELINES

1   Remember what it is you are being asked to describe and do not be sidetracked into writing a vague and rambling piece founded on only one part of the topic.
2   Remember to follow your plan carefully.
3   Develop each part of your plan as fully as possible.
4   For each feature, list a number of *adjectives* to develop your description more fully. The use of adjectives is most important for descriptive essays.
5   Involve all your senses, not just sight – remember sounds, smells and movements. Describe each in as much detail as possible.
6   Make use of *contrasts*. For example, compare a scene by day with a scene by night.
7   Use *comparisons* to enrich your writing. The phrase 'the old man' could be developed into the 'the bad-tempered, fussy old man'.

A descriptive essay, carefully planned and written to these guidelines, is a good choice for you in that your coursework folder will probably have to contain descriptive writing and with thorough practice you will do yourself full justice with this type of writing.

DESCRIPTIONS OF PEOPLE

To describe a person or people well, you will need to use your powers of observation to record these details.

1 Physical features – height, looks, body shape, stature.
2 Clothing.
3 Posture.
4 Speech.
5 Mannerisms.
6 Their job.
7 How they affect other people.

Each of these headings could be the basis for a paragraph, but remember that you are not simply producing a 'Wanted' poster. You will need to make your description come to life and probably the best way to do this is to select those aspects of appearance and personality which are unusual and interesting and develop these more fully in your writing.

Attempt these exercises, using a variety of starting points; i.e. paragraph 1 could be a physical or facial description *or* an aspect of the person's behaviour.

▶ **WRITE DESCRIPTONS OF THESE PEOPLE:**

1 My hero.
2 The oldest person I know.
3 Someone I can't stand.
4 My relatives.
5 Teachers I remember.
6 Myself – ten years from now.
7 Someone I feel sorry for.
8 My (new) neighbour.
9 A best friend.
10 My favourite pop/sports star.

DESCRIPTIONS OF SCENES

If you were given a camera and asked to photograph a country or city scene, you would take a number of pictures. Written descriptions of scenes would take each of these pictures as ideas for paragraphs. Once again, remember the importance of *order* and decide which aspects of the scene you are going to describe. It is worth imagining that you have a TV camera with a zoom lens. You might begin with a broad, general shot and then focus on specific close-ups as in the case of the worked example below. Note again the use of a planning grid.

Example of a descriptive essay plan
The essay title is 'Describe a city scene by day and night' and the essay plan is shown in the grid below.

	DAY	NIGHT
Sounds	traffic bustle people calling a buzz of noise horns blowing	little traffic noise people's conversations heard stillness in the air an alarm bell ringing in the distance
Sights	traffic queues crowds on pavements pigeons on buildings	couples walking home lights in the shops street-lights
Mood	lively frenzied exciting impersonal	deserted eerie lonely

WRITE DESCRIPTIONS OF THESE SCENES

1. The supermarket.
2. The barbecue.
3. School assembly.
4. The take-away.
5. Thunderstorm in the city.
6. The beach – in winter and summer.
7. A country lane in autumn.
8. A frosty night in the country.
9. The scrapyard.
10. My garden.

DESCRIPTIONS OF EVENTS

It is sometimes difficult to distinguish between a narrative and a description here. To combine the two is difficult, but with careful planning there is no reason why you should not manage this successfully. Typical narrative/descriptive essays would be 'Downstream journey' or 'Helicopter flight over my area'. As with the other descriptive essays, remember:

1. Plan the journey.
2. Focus on different parts of the journey, using as much detail as you can.
3. Don't spend too long on one part of the journey.

Example of a narrative/descriptive essay plan
The title is 'A helicopter flight over my area'
Note that four paragraphs form the basis of the essay's organization.

1. Paragraph 1
   * Take-off.
   * Describe sensation of lift-off.

     *   Feelings of fear and anticipation.

2 Paragraph 2
- Gaining height.
- Describe immediate surroundings.
- Everything becomes smaller below you.

3 Paragraph 3
- In flight.
- Contrast colours and scenes.
- Peaceful/busy views, specific detailed descriptions.
- Unusual sights, humorous sights and your reactions.
- Your own house – familiar faces seen from a distance.

4 Paragraph 4
- Touch-down.
- Back to earth on the level again.
- Thoughts and feelings on being back.
- Special memories and reactions to what you have seen.

DESCRIPTIVE ASSIGNMENTS

◇ Work out plans and write paragraphs or full essays on:
1 The storm.
2 Someone I hope I'll never see again.
3 The circus.
4 Harvest time.
5 A view I know well (bring out the features which make it memorable to you).
6 The best/worst lesson I ever had.
7 The most boring event in my life so far.
8 A ceremony in which I have taken part (bring out the nature of the ceremony and your feelings during it).
9 Describe the sights and scenes you encounter on your way to and from work each day.
10 The down-and-out.
11 An area – town or countryside – I know well (bring out its special character).
12 The rock concert.
13 A summer festival.
14 The jumble sale.
15 The dentist's waiting room.
16 The scrapyard.
17 The secret garden.
18 The queue.
19 First girlfriend/boyfriend.
29 Getting away from it all.

DISCURSIVE/ARGUMENTATIVE ESSAYS

This type of essay invites you to express your opinions on certain issues, usually but not always of a topical nature. It follows, then, that you should not tackle this kind of essay unless you know something about the topic in question or have enough research time to obtain information.

PITFALLS

There are two things to look out for:

1   Originality – in your plan you must think of as many original ideas as you can. The examiner will soon be fed-up with stereotyped 'popular' views and credit will be given for new ideas and opinions, as long as they are sensible ones.

2   Pay the usual careful attention to your plan so that you do not get carried away when dealing with one particular aspect of the topic. It is most important that you present a balanced view in both terms of content and depth of treatment.

GUIDELINES

There are several ways to present your opinion on a given topic, but remember that the examiner will be looking for opinions supported by facts and while you may not receive marks for enthusiastic outbursts you will certainly gain marks if you support them with informative facts.

There are two good ways to tackle this type of essay:

1   **Make your own position clear** from the start and present a logical and reasoned argument to support it.

or

2   **Consider both sides** of the question, giving the points for and the points against the topic, leaving your personal opinion until the final paragraph in which you balance the various points on both sides. This is probably the safest way to tackle the essay.

Of all the different types of essay, this is the one where:

1   sensible points, presented in an orderly way;
2   unusual ideas or suggestions;
3   evidence of logical clear thinking and uncomplicated expression;
4   the power with which you argue your case;

will gain you most marks.

Remember, to convince the examiner of your argument, use:

1   facts, figures and statistics designed to impress;
2   language – emotive words and expressions to help the reader to make up his mind.

Example of discursive/argumentative essay plan

The title is 'Smoking', and the planning web is show in Figure 8.

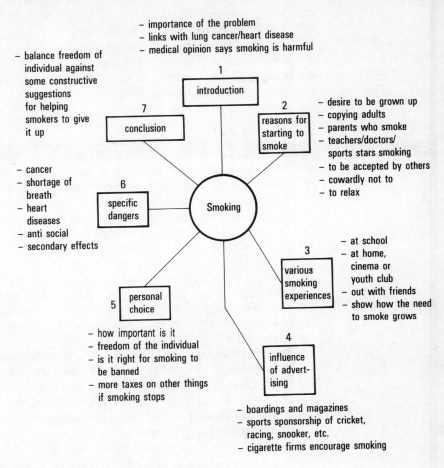

Figure 8 Planning web for 'Smoking'.

DISCURSIVE/ARGUMENTATIVE ASSIGNMENTS

1   Argue for *or* against one of the following:
    *   Public transport should be free to all.
    *   Experiments on animals are necessary for the good of mankind.
    *   You should always tell the truth.

2   'If we go on spending money on arms, there's bound to be a war.' 'I disagree. If a country is strong, no one will dare to attack it.'
    Which of these views seems to offer the better prospect for peace?

3   Present a case for the compulsory study of *ONE* of the following in school or college:
    *   Religious Studies
    *   Politics
    *   English Literature
    *   Art
    *   Computer Studies
    *   Home Economics

4   Is school uniform necessary?
5   What more should be done for disabled people?
6   Should political marches and demonstrations be banned?
7   Should shops be allowed to open on Sundays?
8   What are the arguments for and against our schools adopting the continental day, with an earlier start and finish and NO lunch-break?

PERSONAL/REFLECTIVE ESSAYS

This type of essay offers you the chance to express your own individual personality and very often you are given the opportunity to write from personal experience. Personal writing also lends itself to project or topic work about you or your interests – hobbies, early memories, for example. You may well be asked to include a piece like this in your coursework folder.

PITFALLS

1   You can easily drift off the set topic – with so many personal memories, it is important that you decide which of them you intend to write about.
2   Planning can be more difficult – you must organize your ideas selectively and bear in mind the order of your paragraphing.
3   There is often a tendency to let the pen run away with the story when you write about yourself. There is nothing wrong with this, but do not forget to keep a careful eye on sentence construction and attention to detail.

GUIDELINES

If your memory is jogged and your ideas and recollections come easily to mind, or if you enjoy describing your thoughts and feelings, then bear these points in mind:

1   Your writing is more likely to be lively, interesting and thoughtful if you are writing from your personal memories or thoughts rather than imagined ones.
2   Remember the importance of a sequence of ideas. Decide on an order of paragraphing which seems logical and sensible.
3   When preparing your plan, select those reflections or memories which are especially vivid and clear in your mind and discard any vague or ill-defined recollections.
4   When you begin writing, always give each event background details; don't just launch into 'I remember one summer when . . .' Give the examiner more details. For example:

Where were you?
How old were you?
What do you remember about people, relatives and others who were near?

What about buildings?

What were people wearing?

5   If you follow this method, you will have to be selective in what you choose to describe. The examiner is much more likely to give you a good grade for a few vividly described memories or thoughts than for a disjointed, lengthy and sparsely described list.

Example of a Personal/Reflective Essay Plan

The title is: 'Childhood Memories' and here is a note form plan (see p.40):

1   Paragraph 1 *Introduction*
*   where the memories happened.
*   places and people associated with them.

2   Paragraph 2 *A list of recollections*
*   happy/sad memories.
*   personalities – friends and relations.
*   places visited.
*   some of my most vivid memories were . . .

3   Paragraph 3 *Detailed description of a selection of those memories*
*   choice of three or four.
*   contrasting memories; perhaps 50/70 words on each.
*   make each memory 'live'.

4   Paragraph 4 *Memories which still influence you*
*   way of holding on to memories – photos
*   possessions, etc.
*   how memories affect your actions now.

5   Paragraph 5 *Importance of childhood memories*
*   something to look back on, to share with others.
*   to pass on to your own children perhaps.
*   value of a diary.
*   a base of security in the more turbulent world of adulthood.

PERSONAL/REFLECTIVE ASSIGNMENTS

◊   Prepare plans or full essays on:
1   My most treasured possession.
2   Something about me from a long way back.
3   Write to your future grandchildren, giving an impression of your present way of life, thoughts and feelings as a young person. Consider what they might find interesting to learn about in fifty years' time.
4   Precious memories.
5   One person who made a lasting impression on me.
6   Memorable holidays.
7   Your pet's view of you and your family.
8   Lessons I learned outside school.
9   My place.
10 Getting away from it all – where I go.
11 Myself – ten years from now.

12   What I look for in a friend.

13   My thoughts on (a) religion; (b) parenthood; (c) drugs; (d) sport.

14   What I think makes a good teacher.

15   My guide to babysitting.

16   Some of the things I can't stand.

17   A teenager's guide to moods.

18   My ideas for a peaceful life.

19   Times when I needed a friend.

20   My ideas on changing fashion in clothing and hairstyles.

FACTUAL ESSAYS

If you are sitting an end-of-course examination for GCSE, then you will almost certainly have to produce a number of pieces of writing based on a passage of information. Examples of this type of work are included in the next chapter. However, it is worth noting that these will generally be much shorter than factual pieces of writing produced for coursework – probably within a 100–250 word limit. Your teacher will guide you on the length of essays required for coursework, but 400–600 words could be regarded as average.

In factual essays, you are asked to present detailed information on a definite topic. You may be put off this type of essay because you feel that you do not know enough about the subject in question; or you may know something, but not enough to write perhaps 500 words. You may also find this kind of writing rather boring and prefer to write narratives or descriptions.

However, factual essays can be written from an informed base if you treat them as research projects in which you compile a list of sources of information, extract this information via notes and diagrams and include them in your eventual essay. (Remember to hand in any notes, rough drafts, etc., with your work.)

PITFALLS

1   Remember to keep within the word limits set for the assignment.

2   Be careful with your style of writing – you are writing an explanation.

3   The examiner will most probably not be an expert on the topic in question, but marks will be lost if your facts are seen to be obviously wrong.

GUIDELINES

1   The examiner will greatly prefer a lively and interesting account to a dull recital of complicated facts.

2   He will prefer to be entertained and interested rather than instructed, so break up any potentially dull sections with questions or humour.

3   Do all you can to keep the essay lively and vivid.

4   You will obviously need to go into a lot of detail, but avoid producing a catalogue.

5   Remember that it is better to concentrate on relatively few points and try to say something of general interest and value about each one. Perhaps the most important point to remember is that you are sitting an examination in English language, not political theory, geography or history. While the examiner will obviously be looking to see if you have included a sufficient quantity of information, he will also be scrutinizing the way you have chosen to organize and express it.

Example of a Factual Essay Plan

The title is 'My Hobby'. And here is a note form plan:

1   Paragraph 1 **Name your hobby – cycling**.
     *   Describe how you became interested in cycling.

2   Paragraph 2 **Why cycling interests you now**.
     *   Recreation
     *   Physical fitness.
     *   Chance to see different places.
     *   Freedom of movement.
     *   Little cost.
     *   Chance to enjoy company of others who share your hobby.

3   Paragraph 3 **The technical side**.
     *   Basic maintenance and upkeep costs.
     *   Simple tasks you can do yourself.
     *   Basic repairs.
     *   Some personal memories.

4   Paragraph 4 **Advice for beginners**.
     *   Points to bear in mind when buying a cycle.
     *   Safety on the roads.
     *   Looking after your cycle.

5   Paragraph 5 **Conclusion**.
     *   What cycling can do for you.
     *   Why you have enjoyed it and will continue to do so.

FACTUAL ESSAY ASSIGNMENTS

▷   Draw up a lists of the main points you would include in an essay on some of these topics.

1   Things I value.
2   An account of the recreational opportunities in your area and how you think they might be improved.
3   My kind of music.
4   How to keep a pet.
5   Looking after motorcycles.
6   Flying a kite.
7   A babysitter's manual.
8   Changing the school rules.
9   My route to work.
10   Some do's and don'ts for a weekend job.
11   Computing – how to get started.
12   Equipment for fishing.

13   How to improve a youth club.
14   Camping equipment.
15   Looking after younger brothers or sisters.
16   Television programmes for teenagers.
17   Simple household jobs.
18   A news story.
19   What makes a good teacher.
20   Current 'crazes' – skateboarding, BMX etc.

KEY POINTS FOR FINAL REVISION

	YES	NO
▷ Essay planning		
method 1 (diagram)	☐	☐
method 2 (written)	☐	☐
exercises	☐	☐
▷ Beginnings and endings	☐	☐
— exercises	☐	☐
▷ Paragraphs	☐	☐
— exercises	☐	☐
▷ Narrative essays:	☐	☐
pitfalls	☐	☐
guidelines	☐	☐
structure	☐	☐
characters	☐	☐
— exercises	☐	☐
— planning grid	☐	☐
plan — worked example	☐	☐
twenty assignments	☐	☐
▷ Descriptive essays:	☐	☐
pitfalls	☐	☐
guidelines	☐	☐
describing people	☐	☐
— exercises	☐	☐
scenes	☐	☐
— exercises	☐	☐
events	☐	☐

plan — worked example ☐ ☐

twenty assignments ☐ ☐

◇ Discursive/argumentative essays: ☐ ☐

pitfalls ☐ ☐

guidelines ☐ ☐

eight assignments ☐ ☐

◇ Personal/reflective essays: ☐ ☐

pitfalls ☐ ☐

guidelines ☐ ☐

plan — worked example ☐ ☐

twenty assignments ☐ ☐

◇ Factual Essays: ☐ ☐

pitfalls ☐ ☐

guidelines ☐ ☐

plan — worked example ☐ ☐

twenty assignments ☐ ☐

OTHER FORMS OF EXTENDED WRITING

CONTENTS

64 Contents

In GCSE English you will be given opportunities to use language in different ways, both for your coursework folder and in the 'Response' or 'Expression' examination papers if these are offered at your examination centre. The two aims here are to assess:

1 Your ability to organize material clearly and methodically;
2 Your ability to produce a piece of continuous, lively, imaginative writing, bearing in mind the specified audience and type of writing required.

Here is a list of the possible stimuli you may be offered to get you started:

1 Article – fiction or non-fiction from newspapers, magazines etc.
2 Report – from brochures, booklets, newspapers, magazines etc.
3 Statistical tables – from government or other sources.
4 Maps – town plans, etc.
5 Diagrams – of engineering/industrial processes.
6 Pictures – of people, places or events.

You could be then asked to produce:

1 Different types of report.
2 Letters.
3 Dialogue and plays.
4 Diaries.
5 Poetry.

APPROACHING THE TASKS – GUIDELINES

Remember these points:

1 **Read** the requirements of the task BEFORE you read the article or other starting point. This will help you to direct your reading.
2 **Read** any written extract at least twice (examination time may be set aside for this).
3 **Make a plan** to show the order of the content you intend to include.
4 You will probably be expected to include some material from the extract as well as your own ideas.
5 You will often be asked to write 'in role' – as if you are someone else. The idea here is for the examiner to see how well you can change or adapt your own style of language.
6 You may also be asked to use the same information from the extract, plus your own ideas in writing, for different or imaginary audiences.

7   If you are required to write a factual or informative piece, remember:
*   Be brief and to the point.
*   Write accurately, using given information selectively.
*   Present your material in a logical way.
*   Keep your sentences as straightforward as possible.
*   Remember to use paragraphs.

8   Your end product will be assessed on its *form* as well as its *content* so do read the following more detailed guidelines carefully; familiarize yourself with the traditional methods of organization and layout, especially for letters and dialogue writing.

USING PICTURES, PHOTOGRAPHS, GRAPHS OR TABLES

One of the main differences between GCSE English and the old O levels and CSE English examinations is the increased use which will be made of visual material to get you started. This will include pictures and photographs particularly, but also graphs, tables and statistics.

Very often quite detailed instructions will be offered, particularly if you are being directed to produce certain information as a result of your reading (see Chapter 6, Summary and Directed Writing).

A common introduction to your task, based on a picture or photograph, might be:

> Write a story, description, essay, report or in a style of your own choosing in response to one of the pictures on the accompanying sheet. (Your writing may be directly about the subject of the picture or take some central suggestion from it; there must be some clear connection between the picture and your composition.)

The last part of this instruction is *most important*; you must make sure that your writing has a recognizable link with the picture.

There is no doubt that of all the possibilities for extended writing, a visual starting point gives you greater flexibility in terms of interpretation and the style of writing – story, report, letter, etc. – that you can choose. Apart from the major point mentioned above, if you are going to produce a piece of writing based on a picture or photograph, remember the following;

1   Use the guidelines on extended writing in this Chapter and Chapter 3 on Essay Writing. Note particularly the guidance given on **beginnings** and **endings**.

2   Remember that any **specified word length** for the piece of writing will have to be met.

3   If you choose to write in a narrative style, try to include all the **components** of any picture or photograph. Your teacher or examiner will be looking for your ability to be observant.

4   Don't be afraid to offer a **personal reaction** to what you see. You will be awarded marks for sensitivity.

5 Look, as ever, for an **unusual interpretation** – you will be rewarded for originality.

6 Don't forget that the usual rules of paragraph and sentence construction still apply.

REPORTS

Following your study of the starting point, you could be asked to write different types of report. Here are some examples:

1 A newspaper story
   * crime report
   * accident report
   * sports report.
2 A police report.
3 A holiday report or tourist information brochure.
4 A confidential report or job reference.
5 An eyewitness report.
6 School reports.

A report may be written in two ways:

(*a*) 'First person': written as if you were a *personal participant* in the action – perhaps beginning with 'I', e.g. 'I noticed that the engine was smoking as the car approached the traffic lights . . .'

(*b*) 'Third person': taking a *spectator* view and writing in a detached impersonal way perhaps, e.g. 'The car's engine was smoking as it approached the traffic lights . . .'

GUIDELINES

1 Note whether you are being asked to write a first or third person report.

2 Be sure that you understand the requirements of the task; from whose viewpoint am I writing? for whom am I writing?

3 Read or study the extract/diagram/picture carefully, bearing in mind what you are being asked to do.

4 As you read, underline relevant points or note them on a piece of rough paper.

5 Write a rough plan of the content of the report – remember to use your ideas if this is required.

6 Decide on the order of your content – particularly how you are going to begin and end the piece.

7 Produce a first version or rough draft.

8 Note the number of words (if required to do so).

9 Reproduce a final copy, which should be
   * neat
   * fluent – information should not be 'jerky', so ensure that your ideas are linked.
   * concise
   * to the point

* orderly
* lively and interesting.

PITFALLS

1 The greatest danger is that you misunderstand or misinterpret the task and
   * do not enter fully into the required role of the report writer;
   * ignore the instructions concerning the requirements for the report
2 If you are asked to put your own ideas forward, do remember to include them at the planning stage.

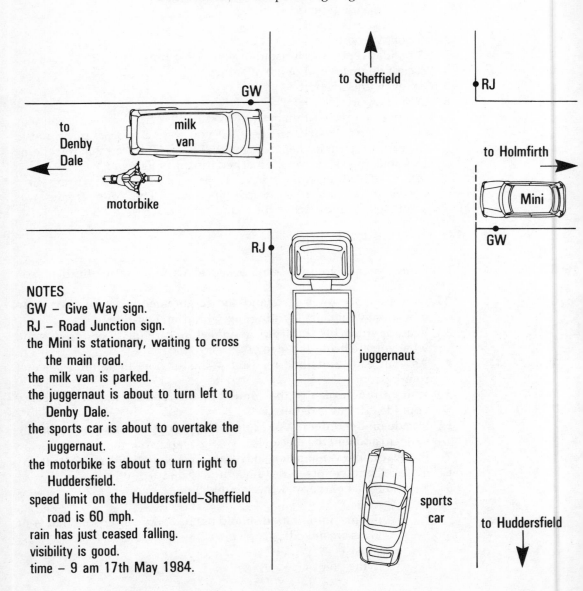

NOTES
GW – Give Way sign.
RJ – Road Junction sign.
the Mini is stationary, waiting to cross the main road.
the milk van is parked.
the juggernaut is about to turn left to Denby Dale.
the sports car is about to overtake the juggernaut.
the motorbike is about to turn right to Huddersfield.
speed limit on the Huddersfield–Sheffield road is 60 mph.
rain has just ceased falling.
visibility is good.
time – 9 am 17th May 1984.

SPECIMEN QUESTIONS

1 ROAD ACCIDENT

An accident took place at the junction of the Denby Dale – Holmfirth Road with the main Huddersfield – Sheffield trunk road. Study carefully the following notes and the diagram which depicts the scene immediately before the crash.

(*a*)   Decide which vehicles actually crashed and if anyone was hurt. Then write the eyewitness account which the driver of the Mini, who had a clear view of the crash, gave to the police.

(*b*)   Write the statements which the drivers of the juggernaut and the sports car gave to the police. The three accounts should be factual and informative but may, of course, conflict and differ about who was to blame.

NOTES
GW — Give Way Sign.
RJ — Road Junction Sign.
The MINI is stationary, waiting to cross the main road.
The MILK VAN is parked.
The JUGGERNAUT is about to turn left to Denby Dale.
The SPORTS CAR is about to overtake the juggernaut.
The MOTOR-BIKE is about to turn right to Huddersfield.
SPEED LIMIT on the Huddersfield – Sheffield Road is 60 m.p.h.
RAIN has just ceased falling.
VISIBILITY is good.
TIME 9 a.m. 17 May, 1984

(Joint Examination Paper, Northern Examining Association)

2 SMOKING

Read the following information lettered (*a*), (*b*) and (*c*) and then argue your case AGAINST smoking. You should try to answer the points made in (*a*) by Martha Middleton and refer to information in parts (*b*) and (*c*) to support your argument. Do not merely copy figures, however. You may include any other relevant information or experience of your own.

(a)   *In defence of smoking Martha Middleton said:*
'I'd be a nervous wreck without my "cigs". It's the same with my husband; he's under so much stress at work. Rather a cigarette than a whisky. Besides I enjoy a good smoke and I can't possibly give up now. It wouldn't do any good. As for lung cancer, my dad lived until he was eighty and he smoked over twenty a day. We've all got to die someday – might as well enjoy ourselves while it lasts, whatever it costs. Besides, think of all the taxes we smokers pay. The Government couldn't do without us, neither could sport. My husband says cricket would be lost without Benson and Hedges!'

(b)   Further Comments.

'The average smoker:

(1)   smokes sixteen cigarettes a day,

(2)   shortens his life by five and a half minutes every time he smokes a cigarette,

(3)   spends over £6 a week on cigarettes.'

Health Education Pamphlet

'The moment you stop your body starts recovering. Five years after stopping smoking the chances of the once-average smoker developing lung cancer are the same as if he'd never smoked at all.'

Chest Specialist

'Pregnant women who smoke threaten the lives of their babies.'

Midwife

'Lung cancer will overtake breast cancer by the end of the 1980s as the biggest killer of women.'

Director of Action on Smoking and Health

'How to stop?

It's really a matter of will-power and sticking with non-smoking friends for a while, but you could try acupuncture or hypnosis. Myself, every time I yearned for a cigarette I did something positive – made myself a drink, washed up or played with the baby.'

Newly successful non-smoking mother

(c)   Statistical Table.

CAUSE OF DEATH AMONG CIGARETTE SMOKERS

Underlying cause of death	Expected deaths[1]	Recorded deaths[2]	Mortality ratio[3]
Cancer of lung	170.3	1,833	10.8
Bronchitis and emphysema	89.5	546	6.1
Cancer of larynx	14.0	75	5.4
Other circulatory diseases	254.0	649	2.6
Cirrhosis of liver	169.2	379	2.2
Coronary artery disease	6,430.7	11,177	1.7
Other heart diseases	526.0	868	1.7
Hypertensive heart	409.2	631	1.5
General arteriosclerosis	210.7	310	1.5
All causes	15,653.9	23,223	1.68

(1) Expected deaths: Figure given shows the number of deaths considered normal among non-smokers.

(2) Recorded deaths: Figure given shows actual deaths recorded among the smokers in the study.

(3) Mortality ratio: Ratio of 2 means that death rate is twice as high for smokers as for non-smokers.

(Source: Adapted from U.S. Department of Health, Education and Welfare, Smoking and Health.)

(Joint Examination Paper, Northern Examining Association)

3   TOURIST BROCHURE

Write a report of 250–300 words for an information brochure on the tourist resort described in note form below. You should decide upon the order in which you wish to present your information.

> *Cawsand* – mild climate – quiet location – near a large town – good beaches – safe bathing – easy road access – close to subtropical parkland – fishing – pony trekking – family accommodation – cliff walks – inexpensive sailing – rock pools.

4

The following are statements made by witnesses to a road accident which occurred near a bus stop, in which a schoolgirl was knocked down by a car. Put yourself in the place of a policeman who has to write a factual report on what happened and who was responsible. Base the report on your interpretation of the information given by the witnesses.

A   *Mr John Black, aged 27 – passer-by:*
'The kid had no chance. The car came speeding up the inside lane, he was just trying to avoid the queue in the other lane. Next thing I knew was that the girl was lying across the bonnet of the Escort. You should have heard the screech of brakes.'

B   *Mr Peter White, aged 41 – Motorist:*
'I was in the outside lane in the line of traffic. The lights were red for traffic travelling straight on along Main Street, but the green filter light was on for traffic turning left up Station Road. The red Ford Escort was coming up the inside lane signalling to turn left when I saw the brake lights on and heard the screech.'

C   *Mr Jim Brown, aged 38 – Bus Driver:*
'Those kids are the same every day. I'm surprised this has not happened before now. They are always running around, chasing each other. I was coming behind the car and I had to brake too. I was doing about 15 m.p.h. so I suppose the Escort was doing the same. He was signalling to go up Station Road. I didn't see the wee girl but there was a crowd of kids at the shop.'

D   *Susan Gray, aged 15 – schoolgirl:*
'It was about 4.15 p.m. and I was waiting for the bus as usual. Sharon wanted to buy sweets at the shop on the other side of the road. She looked around before stepping out. The red Escort AZB 392 just came from nowhere. The driver was sneaking up the inside lane because there was a line of cars waiting at the lights. I think it was shock more

than anything, but she went in the ambulance which I called. I wonder who is going to tell Mrs Green?'

(GCSE Specimen Paper, Northern Ireland Schools Examination Council)

LETTER WRITING

Before you set out to tackle a letter-writing task, it is important for you to familiarize yourself with traditional methods of organization and layout and to be aware of the different demands various types of letters can make.

You may be asked to write one of the following:

1 Personal letter.
2 Official letter.
2 Business letter.

PERSONAL LETTERS

These can be classified into two types:

1 **Formal letters** – usually having a definite purpose such as
  * congratulating a friend on his or her success in an examination, test or promotion.
  * accepting or refusing an invitation to a ceremony, party or wedding.
2 **Informal personal letters** – those which are exchanged between friends and relatives and could be:
  * a description of a holiday or a series of events of common concern.
  * a letter of good wishes or thanks.
  * a letter home.

OFFICIAL LETTERS

These are exchanged between a private person and, for example, an employer, a local government official or anyone else holding an official position.

Such letters could include:

  * letters between landlord and tenant.
  * letters of complaint.
  * demands for payment of bills.
  * letters to the newspaper.

All correspondence involving a private individual and an official matter would come into this category.

BUSINESS LETTERS

These are sent between one company or businessman and another, or between a private individual asking, for example, for a builder's estimate. Other types of business letters could include:

* legal matters.
* contracts and wills
* orders or instructions.

STYLE AND LAYOUT OF LETTERS

Each of the above three types of letter has its own defined style of organization and layout, and it is vitally important for you to remember this when you are writing a letter.

It is **essential** to write in the appropriate **style**; the examiner will want to see if you have done this. You would not, for example, write an informal conversational style of letter to a potential employer. Conversely, you would obviously write in a different way if you were writing to your bank manager requesting a loan, as compared with writing to a friend asking him to attend your New Year party.

The **appearance** of the letter is also important to the examiner and errors in layout, punctuation, spelling and attention to detail will all cost you marks. More detailed guidance on these points will be given in Chapter 7, Accuracy and Attention to Detail. No matter which type of letter you are asked to write, you should think in terms of it having nine parts:

1 Your address.
2 Date.
3 The address of the person to whom you are writing.
4 Greeting.
5 Heading.
6 Text.
7 Signing off.
8 Signature.
9 Postscript (if any).

YOUR ADDRESS

This should be arranged so that it can be read easily. Each part of the address should be on a separate line – these may be staggered or straight. The first line will give the name (if any) of your house; the second will consist of the number of the house and the name of the street, the third will give the village, town or city, followed by the county and finally your postcode.

Your address, at the top right-hand corner of the page, might look like either of these:

(1)	Whispers,	(2)	Whispers,
	14, Spivey Villas,		14, Spivey Villas,
	Petersway,		Petersway,
	Devon.		Devon.
	EX4 3PQ.		EX4 3PQ.

DATE

This can be set out in a variety of ways, but should be put below your address on the right-hand side of the paper. Use commas or full stops if you wish, but there is no real need. You might date your letter:

1 June 9th 1986
2 9 June 1986
3 9.6.86

All are acceptable.

THE ADDRESSEE

The name of the address of the person or organization you are writing to is only required if you are writing an official or business letter. There is no need to put this in personal letters. The address should be written against the left-hand margin, below the date, on the opposite side of the sheet.

GREETING

No matter what you are being asked to write about in the examination letter – whether your mood be affection, hatred, contempt or indifference – it is a long established custom that everyone to whom you write is 'Dear' to you. The word is only very rarely left out in the case of strictly formal letters when a simple 'Sir' or 'Madam' would be used.

HEADING

A heading is really a reference to the subject you are writing about and this is often used in official or business letters. If, for example, you were writing to your local Council regarding their plans to build on some open ground near you, you might head the letter in this way:

Your address
Date

Planning Officer
Council address

Dear Sir,
      <u>Proposed building plans for Vicarage Close</u>

Note that a heading is also used when you are writing a reference, a letter of complaint etc.

THE TEXT

This is the most important part of the letter and so requires greatest attention. Remember these points:

* plan your letter before you write so that things happen logically and chronologically.
* it is customary to begin the text of the letter just to the right of and below the end of the greeting:

Dear Jeanne,

Thanks very much for having us to stay last weekend.

* remember to make the **start** as interesting as possible and always **end** positively.
* use paragraphs to give your letter its structure as well as its appearance; this is especially important when you have to deal with a subject at considerable length. Your reader may be helped if you break up the text into clearly defined sections.
* if you are dealing with a controversial issue, sort out your ideas in an orderly way, get them into the right sequence and then use simple, positive sentences grouped into short, concise paragraphs to press home your argument.
* avoid using over-flowery artificial language.
* be realistic and sincere.

SIGNING OFF

There are **three** commonly used methods of signing off:

* Yours faithfully – when you write official or business letters beginning 'Dear Sir'.
* Yours sincerely ⎤ when you have addressed
* Yours truly ⎦ someone by name.

When writing personal letters you can be as informal as you like when signing off, but the examiner will take a dim view of flippant endings like 'Yours till the pubs run dry'. Expressions like 'Best wishes and love from us all' would be entirely acceptable.

When signing off, note the following:

1 A **capital letter** is needed for the first word of each line of the signing off:

Best wishes
Yours sincerely
Thank you for writing
Yours faithfully.

2 'Yours' needs no apostrophe ('Your's' is *wrong*).

SIGNATURE

A personal letter will be signed in the manner in which you are known to the person to whom you are writing. For more formal letters, it is customary to sign with your usual signature and to print your name underneath it, especially if your signature is difficult to read.

POSTSCRIPT

Do without this if you can. However, sometimes a thought will occur to you, or you will realize that you have left out something from the main body of the text. In these cases write 'PS' underneath your signature (no full stops between the letters) and add your idea. If there is a second idea, write 'PPS' and then do likewise.

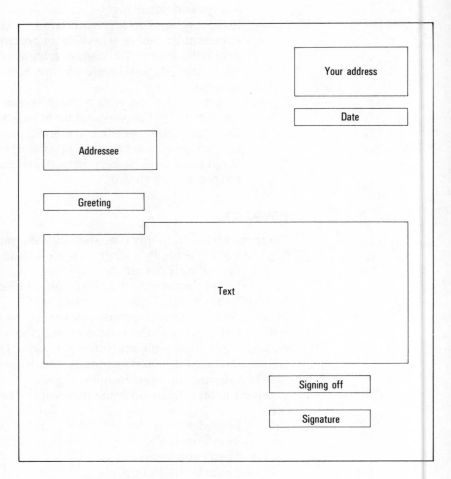

Figure 9 General format for letter.

GUIDELINES   1   Identify the type of letter required and decide on its format.

2   Plan the content you wish to include.
3   Decide on the style and mood of the letter – happy, aggressive, questioning, matter-of-fact etc.
4   Follow the general format in Figure 9.
5   Don't forget to sign the letter.
6   Don't forget to use sentences, paragraphs and correct punctuation.
7   Always find time to check what you have written.

▶ LETTER WRITING EXERCISES

1   Write a letter of complaint to your local newspaper about an increase in bus fares.
2   Write to the manager of a sports shop complaining about the poor wear you have had from a pair of training shoes.
3   Write a letter to a friend about a holiday you have just enjoyed.
4   Write a letter of thanks to a friend whose party you attended.
5   Write a letter to the headmaster of your child's school as a parent who is complaining about the lack of homework being set.

SPECIMEN QUESTION

The following letter appeared in the 'Belfast Telegraph'. Read it and using the correct letter format write a letter to the Editor, Belfast Telegraph, Royal Avenue, Belfast BT1 1EB, giving your response to the points raised.

Thugs run the streets

I am writing to inform you of events which occurred in Belfast City Centre on Saturday last. I hope that by bringing these matters to public attention something will be done to ensure that they do not occur again.

I brought my four-year-old daughter with me into town to do some shopping. As soon as we got off the bus we became aware of crowds of young people, both boys and girls of about 16 years old, standing around corners and in the doorways of some shops. It was clear that some were in gangs of one kind or another by their dress, hairstyles and general behaviour. I was shocked when suddenly they began to run at each other; my daughter was knocked to the ground and, naturally, became very frightened by this stampede. She became quite hysterical and I had to call a policeman to assist us in getting back on to the bus.

This situation cannot be allowed to continue. Decent people cannot come into town while these thugs run the streets. The authorities will have to do something to keep young people off the streets. It is clear that young people of today lack common sense, maturity and consideration for others. Young people of my generation did not behave like this, possibly because their parents had control over them. If parents cannot control their children then it is up to the Government, the City Council and the Police. As a ratepayer, I demand that something should be done.

(Mrs) Joan White

(GCSE Specimen Paper, Northern Ireland Schools Examination Council)

DIALOGUE AND PLAYS

Your teacher will probably give you a number of opportunities to write short dialogues or a scene of a play. These opportunities may well come along as part of your coursework, particularly if this makes up 100 per cent of your mark for the GCSE English examination. You may also be given dialogue or play-writing as an option to choose in a written exam.

The opportunity to write a dialogue or play is usually presented in one of the following ways:

1   In response to a **picture** or **photograph**.
2   As a direct alternative to an essay interpretation of a given title.
3   As a continuation of a piece of written dialogue.

Of these three ways, the *third* is most common; in a written exam question you may also be given detailed guidelines on how you are expected to write your own dialogue. A typical instruction for a timed written answer would be as follows:

> Write a short play by continuing the following dialogue so that the dramatic situation is developed. You are advised as to the method of setting out the dialogue, but do not copy out the extract. You can introduce one or two more characters or add a further scene if you wish.

GUIDELINES

1   You should follow the instruction regarding the setting out of your work. Do not, for example, begin to use punctuation for direct speech if none has been used in the given extract.

2   When you write down everyday spoken language for your dialogue, you are really being expected to use a certain *style* in which certain conventional ways of expressing yourself correctly may be forgotten. In play-writing there are often slang expressions or abbreviated forms of speaking which, when written out, will not appear as sentences. Your teacher or examiner will be ready for this style, however, and you will not be penalized.

3   You should use *stage directions* to help the examiner with the background to the play. These are notes which will be needed to help your play make sense.

4   If you do introduce more characters to assist you in developing your

dialogue, make sure that these are realistic and not too fantastic to be true.

5   Most forms of dialogue or play-writing take a clear story-line and plot and develop them in a special way. Generally, then, these are forms of dramatic *narrative* writing, so do follow the detailed guidance offered in the section on narrative writing (Chapter 3, p.46). In particular, remember that a good start and finish are most important.

6   The examiner will be looking for a clear plot and distinctive characters, so:
*   work out your plan for action beforehand;
*   assemble some notes on each character in terms of appearance, mannerisms, speech style etc.

PITFALLS

1   Do not attempt dialogue writing as part of an assessment until you are confident and practised at it. It is easy to look at it as a slightly softer option than a more conventional type of writing such as an essay, but its demands in terms of plot and characterization are exacting.

2   Remember that the usual requirement in terms of the number of words expected in the finished piece still apply to dialogue.

3   If you do not provide enough signposts to the examiner via stage directions and the actions and speeches of the characters, then your story-line is at risk and the play may end up drifting along without a sense of purpose.

DIALOGUE WRITING EXERCISES

1   (*Stage direction*) A tall, sad and weary-looking young man, carrying an old briefcase, opens the back gate of a small house in the suburbs of the city. As he does so the drizzle turns to heavier rain and he quickens his step towards the front door of the house. As he reaches the door it opens slowly and a bearded and bedraggled old man opens the door.

THE OLD MAN   Go away! It's too soon for this.

STRANGER   Let me in! I'm soaked to the skin.

THE OLD MAN   There's nothing for you here! Clear off.

STRANGER   But you knew I would return.

A WOMAN (who has joined the man at the door) You made your own mind up. How can you expect us to change?

STRANGER   But it's all OK – let me show you.

Continue this dialogue in a manner which develops the dramatic situation. If you wish, you may add a further scene or introduce one or two more characters.

2   You arrive back later than expected from a disco or party. When you open the door someone is there to meet you. Write a dialogue about what happens.

3   A pair of shoes you have recently bought has split along the sole. Write a dialogue between yourself and the manager of the shop when you return with the shoes demanding a refund and he is not at all keen on the idea.

4   The Headmaster has sent for you. When you go into his study he is standing there talking to a parent. Write a three-way dialogue of what happens.

5   A friend has lent you his new motorcycle for the weekend. While it is parked at your home, it is struck by a hit-and-run car. Write the telephone conversation between you and your friend in which you explain what has happened.

6   Write a dialogue between three or four characters in which the first line is, 'Well, who would have guessed it?'

7   Write a scene from a play in which you become involved in a problem on a bus when it is discovered that one of the passengers cannot pay.

8   A young man in overalls knocks on the door, saying that he has come to check on your telephone. You don't trust him, but he insists that he must come in.

9   You lose your direction on a car journey. Write a scene for a play in which there is an unexpected ending.

10 Write a play using one of these ideas:
    *   It was only when I got home from the hairdresser's I realized why they had all gone quiet.
    *   He clearly didn't believe me when I said I was on my way to a fancy-dress party.
    *   I rushed outside when I heard the scream of brakes.

DIARY WRITING

Producing a diary, keeping a record of what has happened to you over a period of time, may well be offered as a possible coursework assignment or examination question. It is a valuable option to consider since it provides you with an opportunity to write from **personal experience** about real or imagined events. Diary writing also has a style and form of its own which is less limiting and restrictive than some more traditional ways of expressing yourself on paper.

GUIDELINES

1   Think of your diary writing as a personal one-way conversation with your best friend. Diary writing at best is nearer in form to spoken language than any other type of written language.

2   The examiner will be looking for lively, original and unusual writing, so don't forget the value of snappy, unusual beginnings such as, 'At last, peace and quiet' and positive endings to conclude a day's entry.

3   Good diary writing for examination purposes should bring in a range of human emotions: happiness, sadness, humour, optimism, gloom etc. Make sure that in its reflection of your real or imagined day's events, your writing contains some of these.

4   The form of expression in diary writing is less governed by conventional punctuation and structure than some other forms of writing, but don't forget that spelling still counts!

5   Diary writing is personal and reflective. It is worthwhile at this stage to read again the section in Chapter 3 on Personal and Reflective Writing (p.56).

6 You must decide on the time span over which the diary will be written. This may well be limited by the required number of words.

PITFALLS

1 Avoid telling a single story, broken up not into paragraphs but by different days. Ensure that there is additional detail each day.

2 Avoid, if you can, a totally fictitious diary. The most effective writing will be done as a result of **direct, personal experience**, so organize your diary around, for example, a significant event in your life, e.g. the first day at a new school or the last day of the holidays.

3 You will lose marks if there is not some degree of balance to your diary in terms of quantity of writing per day, so try to aim at say a half-page minimum for each day, with a little more on some days.

4 A diary should be a **personal commentary on events** in your life. To include a commentary without the events, or vice-versa, will result in a diary of which it would be difficult to make sense, or which could be lacking in originality.

DIARY WRITING – EXERCISES

Use these headings as titles for two to four days of diary entries.
1 Four days I'll never forget.
2 A memorable journey.
3 The beginning and ending of a family row.
4 Visitors – again.
5 My favourite weekend.

POETRY WRITING

Candidates for the O level and CSE English examinations used to be warned against tackling the writing of a poem for examination purposes. The two main reasons for this were:

1 Successful poetry writing is often a way of expressing emotions in a relaxed, peaceful and reflective atmosphere – not in an examination room.

2 Statistically you were likely to get lower marks if you chose to write a poem than if you chose to write an essay.

GCSE English, however, puts much more emphasis on the process of writing and in many cases this will be as important as the final product. The process of poetry writing and its involvement in the production of jottings, notes and rough drafts lends itself particularly well to GCSE, so you are advised to consider the poetry option carefully, especially for coursework.

GUIDELINES

1 Decide on the style and format you wish to use: short/long lines length of verses; any rhyming pattern.

2 Remember that you are trying to paint pictures with your words and expressions, so jot some down before you begin to write your poem.

3 The most sucessful poetry appeals to all our senses – sight, sound, smell, feeling – so consider your topic from these viewpoints at the start.

4 Don't work too hard on rhyme. Many poems are spoiled because of the artificiality of their rhyming patterns. There is a temptation to work too hard to make the wrong word fit at the end of the line and this can so easily spoil the overall effect.

5 It is important to remember that the examiner will usually be more concerned with your ability to express yourself vividly than with your technical expertise in crafting the poem. Form is important, but not as important as your ability to express yourself through images and pictures.

6 Remember to add richness to your vocabulary wherever possible, using a range of adjectives to add colour to your writing,
e.g. the **gnarled and creaking** oak trees, *or*
the **exhausted, distracted** teacher.

PITFALLS

1 You must allow yourself sufficient time to work on rough drafts before coming up with your final version. Your teacher will help you with this. Remember to keep your notes to hand in.

2 It is important that you are **consistent** in your chosen style of expression and layout.

3 Poems can narrate, describe, reflect or discuss. Read the appropriate sections in Chapter 3 to remind yourself of the points made there, especially in terms of content.

▶ POETRY WRITING – EXERCISES

1 Make up a word list as a starting point for poems on these topics:
 * Night-time in the city.
 * The graveyard.
 * Accident.
 * Best friend.
 * My place.

2 Contrast two seasons of the year by focusing on the differences between them in your neighbourhood. Organize these into a poem called 'Contrasts'.

3 Write a humorous poem under the heading 'The day when everything went wrong'.

4 Write a poem in which you recall a memorable incident or event in your life.

5 Write a poem in which you capture one of these feelings or moods:
 * friendship

* sadness

* excitement

* disappointment.

►	**KEY POINTS FOR FINAL REVISION**		
		☐ YES	☐ NO
▷	Starting points for writing task		
▷	Using visual material	☐	☐
▷	Writing reports		
	— First person	☐	☐
	— Third person	☐	☐
▷	Reports		
	— examination questions	☐	☐
▷	Personal letters	☐	☐
▷	Official letters	☐	☐
▷	Business letters	☐	☐
	Letters		
	— style and layout	☐	☐
	— nine points to include	☐	☐
▷	Letter writing		
	— examination questions	☐	☐
▷	Dialogue and plays		
	— guidelines	☐	☐
	— pitfalls	☐	☐
▷	Dialogue writing exercises	☐	☐
▷	Diary writing		
	— guidelines	☐	☐
	— pitfalls	☐	☐
▷	Diary writing		
	— examination questions	☐	☐
▷	Poetry writing		
	— guidelines	☐	☐
	— pitfalls	☐	☐
▷	Poetry writing		
	— exercises	☐	☐

SUMMARY AND DIRECTED WRITING

CONTENTS

During your GCSE course, you may be asked to carry out a variety of different types of summary and directed writing. However, it is unlikely that you will have to spend too much time merely reducing a passage to fewer words and then rewriting it: this type of exercise, known as a précis, has been set less and less often in all types of English examination in recent years.

Summary and directed writing tasks are often set as part of the Expression or Understanding and Response papers set by some examination boards. The tasks fall into two categories, the first generally requiring a more lengthy response.

1 Having read a given passage, you are asked to carry out a piece of your own writing on an identified idea or theme from the passage

   or

2 You are asked to study a passage or passages of argumentative or informative writing which could include pictorial, diagrammatic or graphical information. You are then asked to respond in a variety of ways, including:

   *   summarizing of extracted information under a given heading
   *   note making
   *   letter or report writing
   *   writing argumentatively
   *   developing ideas from the text

In addition to written assignments of this type, there may well be a requirement for you to give short answers in response to questions which test your comprehension or understanding of the text.

Detailed guidance on how to approach this type of task is given in the next chapter.

This part of the GCSE examination will test the following:

1 Your **understanding** of what you have read.
2 Your discrimination and judgement in selecting from it what is **important**.
3 Your ability to **express** this in correct, concise English, using your own words and sentence construction.
4 Your ability to re-present or slant the material according to some particular emphasis for a specified reader or group of readers. This could mean that your writing should convey a mood: e.g. happiness, compassion, embarrassment or sadness.

You will be directly assessed on

1 Orderly, coherent **presentation** of material
2 Use of the appropriate **style**

3 Vocabulary **content**
4 Sound sentence and paragraph **construction**
5 **Accurate** spelling and punctuation.

If a more lengthy response is required, as in category A, then you should use the guidelines offered in the previous chapter on 'Other forms of extended writing' or in Chapter 3 on Essay Writing. Be careful, however, to note the requirements of tasks in terms of mood, audience, number of words etc.

If you are attempting a response in category B – that is, to extract certain specified information from the passage and to rewrite it in a different form – then you should follow these guidelines. Remember that you will be given:

1 **Specific headings** and, therefore, clear key reading tasks.
2 **Detailed guidelines** on how to present your finished product – number of paragraphs, style and mood of writing and specific number of words.

GUIDELINES – SEE FIGURE 10

1 Read the passage through without stopping; re-read it until you have understood it
2 Take a ruler and divide just over one-half of a page into columns for the required number of paragraphs
3 Write the titles of these paragraphs at the top of each column
4 *Either*

*   read the whole passage through slowly once more, making notes in each column under the various headings
        or

*   read the passage through a number of times according to the number of paragraphs headed, looking for the information for each heading.

(The second method is recommended as it is more thorough and you are less likely to miss out any points. If you are working within a specified time limit, however, use the first method.)

5 Once you have assembled your notes, rewrite them in sensible English, in your own words as far as possible, in specified paragraphs.
6 If you are required to do so, count up the number of words used; remember that you should **not** exceed any specified word limit but rather be 10–15 words less than the number prescribed.
7 Finally, rewrite the piece neatly, bearing in mind the required form of the final product; letter, report etc.
8 Remember to rule out rough working and notes, but hand them in with your answer paper. The examiner will see that you have adopted an orderly and systematic approach to the task.

COMMON FAULTS

1   Information included under the wrong headings
2   Main points left out. You can overcome this by underlining the important key sentences in each paragraph – these are often the first sentences in the paragraphs.
3   Regurgitating chunks of the text. Use your own language as far as possible.
4   Lack of coherence and poor expression. A list of all the main points is offered, but their reorganization into a sensible piece of writing is lacking.

Figure 10 Diagram of Working Method for Directed Writing

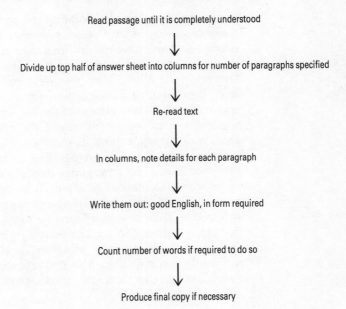

Read passage until it is completely understood

↓

Divide up top half of answer sheet into columns for number of paragraphs specified

↓

Re-read text

↓

In columns, note details for each paragraph

↓

Write them out: good English, in form required

↓

Count number of words if required to do so

↓

Produce final copy if necessary

Directed Writing – Worked Example

You are presented with a 400-word passage which deals with the effect of the introduction of compulsory wearing of seat-belts and you are asked to write two paragraphs under the following headings.

1   The benefits of the compulsory wearing of seat-belts.
2   The disadvantages to the individual of such compulsion.
    You are advised to use no more than 190 words and told that you must only use information presented in the passage.

Benefits	Disadvantages
1 Serious injuries greatly reduced, especially those cause by windscreen smashing. **2** Fewer deaths on the roads. **3** Drivers are more safety-conscious. **4** Increased use of child seat-belts as a result of publicizing 1–3 above. **5** Great saving of hospital time, especially in casualty dept., allowing redeployment of staff to other areas of hospital care.	**1** Some passengers/drivers injured or killed because they have been strapped in and not thrown clear upon impact. **2** Difficulty in freeing some occupants in crashes **3** Freedom of the individual to choose whether or not to wear seat-belt is disregarded. **4** Hospitals increasingly short of spare organs for transplant surgery.

The final version could then be as follows:

Since the compulsory wearing of seat-belts was introduced, the number of deaths and serious injuries caused by road accidents has dropped sharply. Facial injuries as a result of driver and passenger going through the windscreen have been most significantly reduced. Drivers generally are more safety-conscious than before, and the overall number of minor and major accidents has been reduced. The publicizing of this information in newspapers and television has made car users look seriously at the fitting of seat-belts for the rear-seats passengers, especially children. Due to the reduction in number of casualties, it has been possible to transfer staff from some hospitals' accident and emergency departments to work in other wards.

In some accidents, however, passengers have not been thrown clear because they have been strapped in; others have remained trapped by their seat-belts, unable to be freed easily. Above all, many people question the government's right to remove the individual's freedom of choice over whether or not to wear a seat-belt and, although hospitals have fewer road accident victims to attend to, they are now facing an increasing shortage of human organs for transplant surgery. (189 words)

DIRECTED WRITING: SPECIMEN QUESTIONS

1   SCHOOL: A PREPARATION FOR LIFE?

Study the comments below and then discuss how far you think school has prepared you for later life. You should refer to some of these comments, but include ideas of your own in order to develop your argument.

'The idea that being herded together in schools in large competitive groups, unable to escape bullies, is a kind of preparation for life seems especially odd. It is just not true that school is a microcosm of society.'

Journalist

'What we need is more vocational training, more practical subjects, more work experience. I don't care where the money comes from, whether a government scheme or whatever, as long as the training is right.'

Careers adviser

'Computer Studies? What use is that? We can't all be computer programmers. All this nasty technology is taking over our lives. We need protecting from it, not immersing in it.'

Student

'My son needs the best examination grades possible to ensure a good job. He does not need lessons on Life Skills, whatever they might be – sex education, I suppose, leading to more immorality.'

Parent

'One had to cram all this stuff into one's mind, whether one liked it or not. It is nothing short of a miracle that modern methods of instruction have not entirely strangled curiosity.'

Scientist

'I loved school, especially Drama. I remember improvising a scene about Christmas in the trenches in 1914, which not only made me understand the nature of trench-warfare, but also taught me a lot about myself – things I needed to know about myself before I left school. I owe my teachers a lot.'

5th former

'Preparation for life? How can teachers prepare children for life? Most kids are either having a hard time of it now or come from homes that really know how tough life can be. How many teachers can say that?'

Unemployed teenager

'We are preparing children for a world that no longer exists. Schools are expected to uphold values in which society in general no longer believes.'

Headmaster

(Joint Examination Paper, Northern Examining Association)

2 RACIAL PREJUDICE

You have been listening to a school debate on 'Racial Prejudice' in which the following comments were made.

Write your own speech, stating your own views. You should refer to some of these comments, but include ideas of your own in order to develop your argument.

'You meet racial prejudice everywhere. At football matches racialist groups try to recruit hooligan supporters. Disgusting graffiti like 'Hitler was right' or 'Wogs go home' you see scrawled on city walls. Black people live in the worst housing in overcrowded and poor living conditions, and are always insecure. Racialist attacks on their homes and their children mean that some black families live in constant misery and in constant fear.

'Because of language difficulties and cultural differences, immigrant children run a much greater risk of educational failure and thus of employment. Yet if we want a peaceful future, in which men, women and children of different colours and races can live happily together in a just society, schools must point the way. How many of us can honestly say we have tried, really tried, to understand the problems of different ethnic groups?'
Paul

'Really, I think people greatly exaggerate the amount of racial prejudice – especially about jobs. After all, there are coloured doctors and nurses as well as bus drivers and textile workers. Perhaps some blacks don't really try hard enough or expect too much. If some whites are worried that some immigrants keep them out of jobs, that's not racial prejudice; it's natural self-interest.

'It's self-interest, too, that makes people like me concerned about the danger of losing our British identity in a hotch-potch of multi-ethnic cultures. Many immigrants are certainly more than capable of looking after themselves. Racialist attacks are not all one-sided; Asian gangs do sometimes attack innocent whites. Some muggers who fall foul of the law are black.

'I get angry when I'm called a racialist just because sometimes I feel threatened by people who accept all the advantages of living in Britain, but don't seem to want to alter their ways, and sometimes are so alienated themselves that they hardly recognize a friendly hand when they see one – mine, for example.'
Gillian

(Joint Examination Paper, Northern Examining Association)

▶ KEY POINTS FOR FINAL REVISION

		YES	NO
▷	What is being tested	☐	☐
▷	What you will be given	☐	☐
▷	Guidelines	☐	☐
▷	Common faults	☐	☐
▷	Working method	☐	☐
▷	Worked example	☐	☐
▷	Examination questions	☐	☐

COMPREHENSION – UNDERSTANDING AND RESPONSE

CONTENTS

All the GCSE boards require you to answer questions based on your close reading of a passage. The nature of the passage varies. It might be:

1 A piece of fiction or non-fiction, prose or poetry
2 A newspaper report
3 A set of statistics
4 A selection of information

It is common practice for the examination boards to use a variety from this list, especially where two or three passages are used as a basis for questioning.

A comprehension passage will set out to test how well you have understood what someone else has written, and your ability to express that understanding in your own words.

TYPES OF COMPREHENSION QUESTION

The actual questions require different reading comprehension and vocabulary skills and interpretation, but can be broadly defined as requiring the following:

1 **Meanings** of words and expressions used in the passage and your comprehension of them
2 **Reaction** to the passage and **attitude** to its contents
3 **Summary** of information given in different parts of the passage.

Some examination boards describe question types as follows:–

1 **Literal** – finding the fact or giving a definition
2 **Reorganization** – finding the facts and reorganizing them with a response
3 **Inferential** – what do you think the writer is getting at?
4 **Appreciative** – what are your personal reactions to this piece and the ideas in it?
5 **Evaluative** – what is your considered opinion on the issues (you may use other points of reference here).

The examiners usually use categories 1 + 2 in the early part of their questioning to refer to specific words and sentences. Categories 3–5 usually refer to longer passages, paragraphs and sometimes the whole piece of writing. There is in GCSE English a decreasing emphasis on your understanding of words used out of context (dictionary definitions), but an increased demand for you to interpret what the words mean in the sentence or paragraph. It is important for you to realize this.

STYLE OF QUESTIONING

There are two types of questioning used, requiring
1   **Traditional**, written answers.
2   Choice of an answer from a given list (**multiple choice**).

METHOD OF APPROACH

Each style of questioning requires the same initial approach.
1   Read through the passage twice as smoothly as you can; try not to stop at difficult words and expressions on the first reading and do not read beyond the first passage if there is more than one.
2   When you are confident that you have understood the passage, begin to answer the questions in order. Generally, questions follow the order of the text.
3   When you are asked a specific question, read not only the sentence to which it refers but those two or three before and after it. To read a sentence in isolation will often mean a narrow or incorrect interpretation of the question.
4   If you are asked a question on vocabulary, you must ensure that you look at the word **in its context**.
5   If you are asked an inferential, appreciative or evaluative question, you may need to re-read the appropriate paragraph or entire piece again.

WRITTEN ANSWERS

GUIDELINES
1   Always answer in complete sentences – what you say must make sense. Avoid, particularly, beginning answers with 'Because . . .'
2   Refer to the questions – make a link between the question and your answer. Check that you have done this if time permits after you have finished.
3   Take care to follow the instructions in the question.
    e.g.   **In your own words** describe Roger's garden.
            In not more than 200 words give an account of the first day of the family's holiday.
            Find three expressions from the passage which tell us how hard Jill works.
4   Most comprehension questions will show in brackets the number of marks for each question. If time is pressing, ensure that you give most attention to the questions offering highest marks. You should

also vary the length of response according to how many marks are on offer for each question. For example, a question which has 5 marks out of the total of 50 on offer should only need a three- or four-line response.

5 For the more general appreciative questions such as 'How does the writer create a feeling or meaning of ………. in the context?' organize your answer round
* vocabulary: meanings, sounds of words and repetition.
* images and pictures: use of comparisons 'like a . . .'
* detail in focus: 'the twig cracked in the darkness'.
* actions of the characters.

6 Never forget the importance of accurate expression and attention to details of spelling and punctuation (see Chapter 7).

MULTIPLE CHOICE QUESTIONS

You are much more likely to feel the pressure of time when answering a selection of multiple choice questions as part of a written examination paper. Although not all the GCSE boards set multiple choice comprehension examination papers, you may find that your teacher will use such comprehension tests as an objective method of assessing your performance during the course.

As a rough guide, you have usually just under a minute to answer each question, so do not rush. If you find that you cannot answer one question, go on to the next and come back to the unanswered one later.

All multiple choice questions have the following points in common:

1 A number of questions follow each passage.
2 Each full question is divided into the question itself and five possible answers.
3 These answers are presented with letters A, B, C, D, E against them.
4 Only one of these answers is the right one
* you will be asked to write down the *letter* which includes the answer you think is correct.
* you usually have to do this on a separate answer sheet.
5 The other four answers are wrong.
6 Sometimes there may be more than one answer which you feel should be 'correct'. You will then have to choose not only between the right and wrong answers, but also between the probable and **most** probable answer.
7 All the questions will be linked to the context, ideas and presentation of the passage. You must always base your answers on what is in it, **not** on your own ideas or opinions.

GUIDELINES

1 Read each question carefully until you understand its requirements. Having done so, you may find it helpful to ask yourself, 'What am I looking for?'

2 Re-read the section of the passage to which the question refers (you will often be given line references).

3 Read through the five answer options.

4 Evaluate each one carefully.

5 One or more wrong answers may be easy to identify and eliminate from your selection.

6 If your choice is then a difficult one, remember that your answer must relate to the context.

7 Mark your answer sheet as instructed – remember to write down the letter and not the complete answer. Also remember that only **one** answer is acceptable.

8 If any item seems too difficult, do not lose too much time puzzling over it; move on to the next question and come back to the difficult one later if time permits.

9 Above all, do not lose heart if you cannot work out the key answers to consecutive questions. Stop, relax and re-read the passage to which the items refer.

10 Do not panic. Approach the task as calmly as possible and remember that confidence and success in this part of the English Language examination depend on your practice of the techniques outlined above.

Remember, when faced with a multiple choice test, that it is important not only to have a good general understanding of the whole text, but also a clear understanding of the paragraph or group of sentences upon which each question is based.

Finally, it makes sense to put in a response to every question, so while it is important that you should not arrive at your answer by guesswork, if you are running out of time, don't be afraid to go back over your answer sheet and make sure that each question has a response.

LOW MARKS FOR COMPREHENSION

There are five reasons why you may fail to do yourself justice in comprehension questions:

1 Failure fully to understand the passage.

2 Failure to read the passage carefully.

3 Careless reading of the question.

4 Failure to match the question to the part of the passage to which it refers.

5 Failure to use your own words to express ideas from the passage.

PART 1

Read the following passages. Both give accounts of teenagers meeting some old people. As you read, you should consider the following:

    each person's behaviour, feelings and attitudes towards the old people;

    the old people's feelings about them;

    and the ways in which things are described.

You will be asked questions on these points in Part II.

You have fifteen minutes' reading time. You may make notes on details of the passages in your answer book.

Passage One

The person keeping the diary is Adrian Mole, aged 13¾.

Sunday July 4th.

FOURTH AFTER TRINITY. AMERICAN INDEPENDENCE DAY.

I was just starting to eat my Sunday dinner when Bert Baxter rang and asked me to go round urgently. I bolted my spaghetti Bolognese down as quickly as I could and ran round to Bert's.

    Sabre, the vicious Alsatian, was standing at the door looking worried. As a precaution I gave him a dog choc and hurried into the bungalow. Bert was sitting in the living room in his wheelchair, the television was switched off so I knew something serious had happened. He said, 'Queenie's had a bad turn.' I went into the tiny bedroom. Queenie was lying in the big saggy bed looking gruesome (she hadn't put her artificial cheeks or lips on). She said, 'You're a good lad to come round, Adrian.' I asked her what was wrong. She said, 'I've been having pains like red-hot needles in my chest.'

    Bert interrupted, 'You said the pains were like red-hot knives five minutes ago!'

    'Needles, knives, who cares?' she said.

    I asked Bert if he had called the doctor. He said he hadn't because Queenie was frightened of doctors. I rang my mother and asked her advice. She said she'd come round.

    While we waited for her I made a cup of tea and fed Sabre and made Bert a beetroot sandwich.

    My mother and father came and took over. My mother phoned for an ambulance. It was a good job they did because while it was coming Queenie went a bit strange and started talking about ration books and stuff.

Bert held her hand and called her a 'daft old bat'.

The ambulance men were just shutting the doors when Queenie shouted out, 'Fetch me pot of rouge, I'm not going until I've got me rouge.' I ran into the bedroom and looked on the dressing table. The top was covered in pots and hair nets and hairpins and china dishes and lace mats and photos of babies and weddings. I found the rouge in a little drawer and took it to Queenie. My mother went off in the ambulance and me and my father stayed behind to comfort Bert. Two hours later my mother rang from the hospital to say that Queenie had had a stroke and would be in hospital for ages.

Bert said, 'What am I going to do without my girl to help me!'

Girl! Queenie is seventy-eight.

Bert wouldn't come home with us. He is scared that the council will take his bungalow away from him.

Thursday July 29th

My father has been working flat out on the canal bank for the past three days. He hasn't been getting home until 10 p.m. at night. He is getting dead neurotic about leaving it and going on holiday.

Went to see Queenie in hospital. She is in a ward full of old ladies with sunken white faces. It's a good job that Queenie was wearing her rouge, I wouldn't have recognized her without it.

Queenie can't speak properly so it was dead embarrassing trying to work out what she was saying. I left after twenty minutes, worn out with smiling. I tried not to look at the old ladies as I walked back down the ward, but it didn't stop them shouting out to me and waving. One of them asked me to fetch a nice piece of cod for her husband's tea. The tired-looking nurse said that a lot of the old ladies were living in the past. I can't say I really blame them; their present is dead horrible.

Sunday September 19th

FIFTEENTH AFTER TRINITY

Took a deep breath and went to see Bert and Queenie today. They were hostile to me because I've neglected them for a week.

Bert said, 'He's not bothered about us old 'uns no more, Queenie. He's more interested in gadding about.'

How unfair can you get? I can't remember the last time I gadded about. Queenie didn't say anything because she can't speak properly because of the stroke, but she certainly looked antagonistic.

Bert ordered me to come back tomorrow to clean up. Their home help comes on Tuesdays and Bert likes the place to be tidy for when she comes.

Sunday November 7th

Went to see Bert and Queenie with my mother.

Everyone we met on the way asked my mother when the baby was due, or made comments like, 'I expect you'll be glad when the baby's here, won't you?'

My mother was very ungracious in her replies.

Bert opened the door, he said, 'Ain't you dropped that sprog yet?'

My mother said, 'Shut your mouth, you clapped-out geriatric.'

Honestly, sometimes I long for the bygone days, when people spoke politely to each other. You would never guess that my mother and Bert are fond of each other.

Everyone was too old, or too ill, or too pregnant to do any cooking (I developed a sudden ache in both wrists). So we ate bread and cheese for our Sunday dinner. Then, in the afternoon we took it in turns to teach Queenie to speak again.

I got her to say, 'A jar of beetroot, please', dead clearly. I might be a speech therapist when I grow up. I have got a definite flair for it. We got a taxi back home because my mother's ankles got a bit swollen. The taxi driver moaned because the distance was only half a mile.

Passage Two

It was mid-morning – a very cold, bright day. Holding a potted plant before her, a girl of fourteen jumped off the bus in front of the Old Ladies' Home, on the outskirts of town. She wore a red coat and her straight yellow hair was hanging down loose from the pointed white cap all the little girls were wearing that year. She stopped for a moment beside one of the prickly dark shrubs with which the city had beautified the Home, and then proceeded slowly towards the building, which was of whitewashed brick and reflected the winter sunlight like a block of ice. As she walked vaguely up the steps she shifted the small pot from hand to hand; then she had to set it down and remove her mittens before she could open the heavy door.

'I'm a Campfire Girl . . . I have asked to pay a visit to some old lady,' she told the nurse at the desk. This was a woman in a white uniform who looked as if she were cold; she had close-cut hair which stood up on the very top of her head exactly like a sea wave. Marian, the little girl, did not tell her that this visit would give her a minimum of only three points in her score.

'Acquainted with any of our residents?' asked the nurse. She lifted one eyebrow and spoke like a man.

'With any old ladies? No – but – that is, any of them will do,' Marian stammered. With her free hand she pushed her hair behind her ears, as she did when it was time to study Science.

The nurse shrugged and rose. 'You have a nice multiflora cineraria there,' she remarked as she walked ahead down the hall of closed doors to pick out an old lady.

There was loose, bulging linoleum on the floor. Marian felt as if she were walking on the waves, but the nurse paid no attention to it. There was a smell in the hall like the interior of a clock. Everything was silent until, behind one of the doors, an old lady of some kind cleared her throat like a sheep bleating. This decided the nurse. Stopping in her tracks, she first extended her arm, bent her elbow, and leaned forward from the hips – all to examine the watch strapped to her wrist; then she gave a loud double-rap on the door.

'There are two in each room,' the nurse remarked over her shoulder.

'Two what?' asked Marian without thinking. The sound like a sheep's bleating almost made her turn round and run back

One old woman was pulling the door open in short, gradual jerks, and when she saw the nurse a strange smile forced her face danger-ously awry. Marian, suddenly propelled by the strong impatient arm of the nurse, saw next the side-face of another old woman, even older, who was lying flat in bed with a cap on and a counterpane drawn up to her chin.

'Visitor,' said the nurse, and after one more shove she was off down the hall.

Marian stood tongue-tied; both hands held the potted plant. The old woman, still with that terrible, square smile (which was a smile of welcome) stamped on her bony face, was waiting . . . Perhaps she said something. The old woman in bed said nothing at all, and she did not look round.

Suddenly Marian saw a hand, quick as a bird claw, reach up to the air and pluck the white cap off her head. At the same time another claw to match drew her all the way into the room, and the next moment the door closed behind her.

'My, my, my,' said the old lady at her side.

Marian stood enclosed by a bed, a washstand and a chair; the tiny room had altogether too much furniture. Everything smelled wet – even the bare floor. She held on to the back of the chair which was wicker and felt soft and damp. Her heart beat more and more slowly, her hands got colder and colder, and she could not hear whether the old women were saying anything or not. She could not see them very clearly. How dark it was ! The window blind was down, and the only door was shut. Marian looked at the ceiling . . . It was like being caught in a robbers' cave, just before one was murdered.

Part 2

Passage One

1 Describe in detail Queenie's 'turn' and what happens to her after-wards.

2 What do you learn about Adrian Mole's behaviour, feelings and attitude towards Bert and Queenie from the way he treats them?

Passage Two

3   What impressions are given of the atmosphere and conditions of the Old Ladies' Home?

4   Imagine that Marian keeps a diary. Write her diary entry for the days she visits the Home. Include the important things that she notices and what she feels about them. Bear in mind that a diary entry need not be too long (see Adrian Mole's).

Both Passages

5   Imagine that you are an elderly person reading these two passages. Give your impression of the two young people involved.

(GCSE Specimen Paper, London and East Anglia Board)

Read the story and then answer the questions which follow.

JANE IS A GIRL

He hastily gulped the tea remaining in his cup, grabbed the piece of bread and jam from his plate, started to stuff it into his mouth as he rose from the chair and was stopped by his mother's voice: 'Sit down! Where are you going?' and as he went to answer: 'Don't talk with
5   your mouth full!'

Jude thought she was most unreasonable.
'Now?' she queried, when she saw he had swallowed the bite.
'Out,' he said.
'Mother,' she said automatically.
10 'Mother,' he said.
'Be in here at eight o'clock,' she said. 'Not a minute after. Don't have me chasing you or you'll feel the weight of my hand.'
'All right,' he said, moving.
'Mother,' she said.
15 'Mother,' he said.
'Will I ever put manners into you?' she asked the ceiling.
He was going the back way into the yard from the kitchen, when he stopped and thought. Then he turned and ran up the stairs. He went into a room there. His big brother was in front of the mirror brushing
20 his hair.
'Give us a tanner, Joe,' he suggested.
'Get out of here,' said Joe. 'I want all my tanners.'
'Spending them on old girls,' said Jude.
He banged the door and ran. Joe didn't chase him. At the foot of the

25   stairs he went into the other bedroom. His sister screamed. She was
only half-dressed.
'How dare you come into a lady's room without knocking?' she
shouted, hurriedly covering herself.
What a stupid fuss about nothing, Jude thought. 'Give us a tanner,
30   Nora?' he asked.
'What do you want sixpence for?' she asked. 'Don't use slang.'
'Sweets,' he said.
'I can only give you tuppence,' she said. 'It's all I can afford.' She
reached for her handbag.
35   'Oh, all right,' he said, holding out his hand.
'Go and wash that dirty hand,' she said, putting the pennies into it.
'All right,' he said. 'You smell nice.' He said this just to please her. He
didn't like all the scents, but that wasn't too bad.
'Close the door after you,' Nora said.

40   He did so, and went to the sink in the yard and washed his hands
with the big bar of white soap. He didn't want to go back into the
kitchen for the towel, so he just went out the back way shaking his
hands to dry them.

He went around the corner into the small market-place. There was a
45   shop there. Jude looked into the window. He decided on bull's-eyes
which were eight a penny. Each one, uncrunched, lasted for five to
ten minutes. That meant nearly two hours of minty sweetness if you
gave away only four at the most.

Jude took one from the bag and put it under his tongue. This was the
50   best way to make it last. He went back to his street. It seemed empty,
houses on one side facing houses on the other side, their front doors
opening on to the pavements. The people were hidden by lace cur-
tains and geraniums in pots. It was a Sunday evening in March.
Jude hoisted himself on the wide window-sill of one of the houses.
55   He knew this was a house where they didn't mind you sitting on the
window-sill. Others did. They would roar at you, frightening the life
out of you if you weren't anticipating it.

He now shifted the sweet from under his tongue to his cheek and
made it bulge there. He knew this would attract custom because,
60   although there didn't seem to be a living soul inhibiting those houses,
there would be small eyes watching the street.
Sure enough four playmates to use his sweets on. There were several
games they could play. Marbles were not in season, so it would have
to be rounders at the four corners where one street bisected the other.
65   On the whole he decided they would play hurling. It was more
exciting and would warm him up on a cold evening, so when Jane
came out of the house, he took the bag of sweets out of his pocket and
looked into it. That brought her. 'Have a sweet,' he said, handing her
one. She took it, so he knew she was enrolled. Pat Fane, Jonjo and

70   Tip Heaney were the other three, so they leaned against the wall,
     sucking carefully at their sweets. Some of the smaller children also
     arrived and sat on the kerb or stood with their hands behind their
     backs, looking, and their mouths watering. Jude knew this was
     slightly cruel, but how could he dish out sweets to all of them?

75   He got off the window-sill, crunched his sweet to bits and said: 'We
     will play hurling.' They considered this for a moment, and then they
     ran. He ran himself down the street, around the backs of the houses,
     into his own yard where he picked up the hurley stick and soft rubber
     ball. When he got back to the street, the others were scurrying about.
80   His own hurling stick was in good shape. The boss had been broken,
     but he had repaired it with a band of tin that came wrapped around
     fruit boxes. Jane had a good hurley stick, too, better than his own.
     The others had makeshift hurleys that were mostly bits of stick with a
     crude curve at the end, but they were well used and as precious to
85   them as if they were due to play in an all-Ireland hurling final.

     He picked his team. He took Tip Heaney who was the biggest of them
     and a bit rough, while Jane had Pat Fane and Jonjo. They divided the
     small ones up between them. The boys took off their coats and put
     them on the ground to act as goalposts. They sent two of the smallest
90   to each end to watch out for the police, because at this time some
     some of the people took to talking in the Council about the way you
     couldn't walk the streets of the city without being belted with balls or
     knocked down by racing kids. Hadn't they homes to go to or the wide
     spaces of the municipal playing fields? All that stuff, so you had to
95   post sentries.
     Jane and himself put the ball in the middle of the street. Then they hit
     their hurleys on the ground, clashed them three times and then
     scrambled for the ball. The game was on. It was vigorous. It was
     interrupted once or twice when irate mothers ran out to take their
100 children's best Sunday clothes from the dusty road, brushing them
     angrily, and shaking their fists before departing. They replaced the
     lost goalposts with rocks. Once the ball hit a window and all of them
     stood like statues waiting for the result, ready to run if the reaction
     was hostile. Nothing happened, so they continued to play.

105 Jude's side was being defeated. The combination of Jane, Pat Fane
     and Jonjo was too powerful. Jude himself was fast and slick, but Tip
     was too slow and heavy, and even the little tricks he used like putting
     the hurley between his opponent's legs to trip him were unavailing in
     the end.

110 So they had to take to argument. It was a goal! It wasn't a goal! It went
     outside the stone. Didn't it? Yes it did! No it didn't! You stupid idiot,
     are you blind? The veins in their necks stood out as they tried to
     outshout one another.
     This led to a lot of heat and a lot of vigour. It developed into a furious

115   struggle between Jude and Jane. Each time the ball came to them, they slashed and heaved and threw their bodies at one another until one got the victory and belted the ball away. Sometimes Jane won those struggles and sometimes Jude, and they glared at one another like animals. Now! See! I told you! Jude had cuts on his knees and
120   Jane's stockings were torn. They were egged on by the others. The street was a canyon of shrill screams and shouts being deflected into the sky.

    This last time the ball was in the air, and they were pressing together looking up, watching its descent. They raised their hurleys to catch it.
125   It came down between them, the ball escaped and Jude fell on top of her.

    Now as he fell, shouting, his forehead was practically touching hers. He could see her wide eyes and the bead of sweat between her eyebrows and her white teeth snarling at him from drawn-back red
130   lips. Something happened between them. He saw her face changing as she looked up at him, the excitement dying out of her eyes. He was conscious of feeling different inside himself. This game he had engineered no longer mattered. He was suddenly very conscious that the shape of her body was different from his own.
135   This is when it came into his mind: Why, Jane is a girl! Jane is a girl! He was suddenly embarrassed. His face was red from exertion before. Now it seemed to him to get redder. He got to his feet. She got up too. She avoided his eyes.
    Jude couldn't stand this any longer. He turned and walked away
140   from the field. They were stunned. They called after him: 'Hey, Jude! Where are you going? Hey, Jude!'
    He was in an agony of embarrassment. He was upset. He wanted to run, but this would look bad. Instead he took the bag of sweets from his pocket, looked at it and threw it towards them. The bag burst and
145   the sweets flew all over the place. They stopped calling then and scrambled for the sweets, laughing. Jane didn't. She had gone to the path and stood there with her back turned. Did she feel the same? he wondered. Did she say, why Jude is a boy?

    He went in the back way to his house. He put his hands under the
150   tap. He filled his palms and sloshed the cold water on his face. His face was hot. He washed the blood from his knee cuts so that his mother wouldn't be fighting about them. Then he went into the kitchen. There was nobody there. He sat on the wooden stool in front of the fire, rested his elbows on his knees, his chin on his hands, and
155   he thought. Why should it be different? he wondered. What difference does it make? Now he could see that she had long hair, that she wore dresses, that she was good-looking, but she was a Girl. Wasn't she always one? What was the difference now? Now that he came to think of it Pat Fane was also a girl, and she had fair
160   hair.

'Are you sick or something, Jude?' his mother asked. 'Sitting there gazing into the fire. Why aren't you out playing?' He thought he might tell her. But then he didn't. She was always very busy. She sat sewing and listening to the radio. There was a knock at the front door
165 and she put down the sewing and went to answer it.

His sister came down to the kitchen now, ready to go out. She was all dolled up. She looked at the silent boy.
'What's wrong, Jude?' she asked.
'Jane is a girl,' said Jude, thinking she would understand.
170 'Say that again,' she said.
'Jane is a girl,' he said.
'Well, what did you think she was, a rhinoceros?' she asked.
'Hey, Joe, Joe!' she was calling. 'Come here while I tell you!'
'No, no!' pleaded Jude.
175 Joe came downstairs fixing his tie. Nora was laughing.
'Guess what?' she asked. 'Jude has discovered that Jane is a girl.'
'What, at his age? Not even twelve,' said Joe.
Then she was calling her mother.
'Mother, come here while we tell you what Jude said.'
180 Jude fled, his face flaming, towards a green field, as if he was being pursued. He threw himself on the grass. Nobody could find him. He turned on his back and looked at the sky. It was darkening already. There were colours around its edges.

They don't understand, he raged, gripping the grass with his fingers.
185 How could you make them understand and not to be laughing? He remembered going into his sister's room for the pennies. She had covered herself up. She was a girl too, see. Before it had made no difference. Now things were changed. They would never be the same. Never again.

1 Look at lines 1–43. Describe Jude's home and family.

2 Look at lines 25–75.
   For what reasons is Jude so keen to get money?

3 Look at lines 44–104. Describe the kind of neighbourhood where Jude lives.

4 Look carefully at the way the writer describes the game of hurling from its start (line 96) to the time when both Jane and Jude miss the ball (lines 124–126). By commenting on words and phrases used, show how the writer convinces you that the game meant a lot to the children, and particularly to Jane and Jude.

5 What effect does the discovery that Jane is a girl have on Jude's behaviour, thoughts and feelings?

6 Study carefully the relationship between Jude and his mother

throughout the story. Then write what you think of her as a mother, supporting your views with evidence from the story.

(GCSE Examination Paper, Northern Examining Association)

KEY POINTS FOR FINAL REVISION		
◊ Starting points	☐ YES	☐ NO
◊ Types of question	☐	☐
◊ Style of questioning	☐	☐
◊ Method of approach – general	☐	☐
◊ Written answers: guidelines	☐	☐
◊ Multiple choice answers – guidelines	☐	☐
◊ Five reasons for low marks in comprehension	☐	☐
◊ Comprehension examination questions	☐	☐

ACCURACY AND ATTENTION TO DETAIL

CONTENTS

It is common practice for the GCSE examiners to remind you of the importance of good presentation, expression, spelling, punctuation and grammar with such statements as:

'Careless and untidy work will be penalized.'

or

'You are reminded of the necessity for good English and orderly presentation in your answers.'

PRESENTATION

It is clearly in your best interest to present your work so that it can be read easily, so remember these points:

1 Practise your handwriting if it is scruffy and difficult to read.
2 Stick to one style of handwriting.
3 Indent paragraphs in a consistent way. Begin them approximately one inch from the left-hand margin.
4 Write slowly and clearly, remembering that the examiner may well be tired when your script comes to be marked and will not be well disposed towards slipshod handwriting and layout.

EXPRESSION

It is vital that what you write should be clear and understandable to the reader. It is no use having the most original and exciting ideas if you are unable to pass them on to anyone else; similarly, it is of little use if you know the answer to a question, but cannot express it clearly. Accuracy is another essential factor, especially in essay writing. The examiner may well pardon the odd lapse in expression, but you will certainly lose marks if your work contains repeated inaccuracies. Some of the worst faults that examiners find are in

1 sentence construction
2 paragraph construction

SENTENCES

Three common faults:

1 Construction ignored, with basic rules not followed:

e.g.   What did I see? A mass of roundabouts. A dazzle of side-shows. A ragged crowd of people. A buzz of noise.

There is nothing wrong with the vocabulary used, but this succession of phrases has no verbs to give linked order.

2   Sentences lack variety in length and construction:

e.g.   I heard a crash. I went into the bedroom. Richard was playing cricket there. I saw the broken window. I couldn't see the cricket ball.

There is nothing grammatically wrong with any of these sentences, but together they offer a very stilted and jerky read to the examiner. Use commas to join sentences and vary the sentence length.

3   Sentences are so long and complicated that the examiner cannot understand the meaning.

When writing sentences, the important points to remember are as follows:

1   Vary the length and shape of your sentences. Aim at a balance between long and short sentences.

2   Use short sentences:
*   when you wish to express pace or speed of action;
*   to break up an otherwise monotonous collection of longer sentences.

3   When using long sentences beware of:
*   making the sentences over-complex;
*   losing the original meaning;
*   trailing away into inconclusive insignificance.

4   Another useful way of presenting the examiner with a variety of sentence structure is to use a technique called **inversion**. Instead of writing, 'I saw a wisp of smoke on the horizon', you could write, 'On the horizon I saw a wisp of smoke'. Don't overdo this technique, however.

PARAGRAPHS

Examiners also find common faults in paragraph organization:

1   The whole essay is written in one huge paragraph.

2   The writing is organized into dozens of tiny paragraphs, many of them consisting of only one sentence.

3   Lines are missed between paragraphs.

4   There is no consistent pattern of layout. Some paragraphs begin below the final word of the last sentence, while others begin at – or are inset from – the margin.

5   The common errors of sentence construction can also be applied to paragraph organization. You will most certainly lose marks for work that is characterized by extremes.

Important points to remember are as follows:

1   The way of planning your work outlined in Chapter 3 should give you the detailed method of expressing your ideas in paragraphs.

2   If your writing is characterized by one or more of the faults listed

above, do spend time listing and organizing your ideas prior to writing.

3   A good essay will contain:
*   a limited number of paragraphs – perhaps six or seven;
*   paragraphs of a reasonable length;
*   paragraphs each one of which consists of material about one topic.

PUNCTUATION

Many candidates in English examinations lose marks for incorrect punctuation, particularly in essays and other types of extended writing. Punctuation is available to help you convey meaning in what you say.

Many of the traditional rules of punctuation have changed or been adapted in recent years, but their main purpose is still to show groupings of words and the different emphasis you wish to give.

CAPITAL LETTERS

These are used for the first letter of
*   The first word of a sentence.
*   The first word of direct speech, e.g. He said, 'Come here.'
*   All proper nouns and adjectives – names, e.g. John, London, Australia, English.
*   The months and days of the week.
*   The first and all other important words of titles: e.g. I saw *A Hitchhiker's Guide to the Galaxy*.
*   The interjection 'O' and 'Oh' and the pronoun 'I'.

PUNCTUATION MARKS

The following punctuation marks are used in English:
1   .   full stop
2   ,   comma
3   ;   semi-colon
4   :   colon
5   :–   pointer
6   ?   question mark
7   !   exclamation mark
8   '. . .' or ". . ."   inverted commas (speech marks)
9   ( ) or [ ]   round or square brackets
10   —   dash
11   '   apostrophe
12   -   hyphen

The full stop, comma, semi-colon and colon are written or printed signals which help us to organize particular groups of words in a way which enables them to make sense.

Brackets, dashes, inverted commas, quotation and speech marks show a particular type of interruption.

Question marks and exclamation marks are used at the end of sentences to give the proper mood or emphasis.

Apostrophes and hyphens are used to clarify meaning.

FULL STOPS

A full stop is used when you want your flow of meaning to stop. Be careful:

1 *not* to use a comma instead of a full stop at the end of sentences;
2 to follow your full stop with a capital letter if you are beginning a new sentence.

A full stop is used, then:

1 At the end of sentences which are neither questions nor exclamations,
e.g. It was time for John to go to bed.
2 At the end of a group of words, which although not a sentence is a separate sense unit such as in a letter or note,
e.g. Vicarage Road,
     Bristol.
3 In abbreviations or when words are shortened:
O.H.M.S (On Her Majesty's Service)
B.A. (Bachelor of Arts)
Hon. Sec. (Honorary Secretary)
There is a tendency to leave out full stops (a) if the abbreviation ends with the same letter as the shortened word, e.g. Doctor – Dr or Mister – Mr; (b) if the abbreviation becomes an accepted word, e.g. BBC.

◆   EXERCISES

◇   Write out the following, putting in the capital letters and full stops.
1   we went to france for a holiday in august it was very hot and sunny
2   steve evans moved very slowly last Wednesday he had an injured leg this made him run even more dangerously than usual
3   jeans greenhouse at coombe park was full of tomatoes she watered them every day and had so many that she took them to kingsbridge to sell them

COMMA

Commas are used when a brief pause seems required and are used inside sentences. *They are not replacements for a full stop.*

The have four main uses:

1 To divide up parts of a sentence. Note that the sentence could still make sense if the words within the commas were left out. Examples:
*   Mr Smith, our history teacher, has now retired.
*   This car, in the next week or so, needs a service.

> The children, frightened by the pantomime, have had dreams all night.

2 To separate the name of the person being spoken to from what is said. Examples:
> * Sue, are you off to tennis now?
> * Why did you throw that stone, Tom?
> * Johnny, do sit down.
> * Did you know, Harry, that your van has a puncture?

3 To separate direct speech when the verb of saying is involved.
> * 'Come in now,' said Peter, 'it's time for bed.'
> * 'We all know that,' he said. 'Try another question.'

4 To separate items in a list (note that it is **not** usual to use a comma if 'and' joins the last two words).
> * Teachers, students, parents and friends.
> * In the drawer John found a penknife, some postcards, photos and an old camera.
> * The sea was calm, shimmering, inviting and nearby.

COLONS AND SEMI-COLONS

Colons and semi-colons are punctuation marks which are difficult to use correctly. However, they are valuable tools for controlling long sentences, although they should be used with care.

A colon connects sentences or statements. It is weaker than a full stop, but stronger than a comma.

Colons are used:

1 To introduce a list.
> * I will need some equipment for the examination: pen, pencil, a ruler and a rubber.

2 To link ideas to an immediately previous statement.
> * Cricket is not merely a game: it is a way of life.

3 Before a list of statements which develop and expand on a single theme.
> * I looked at the new house: the carpet was clean, the cupboards shining and the walls newly painted.

4 To begin or introduce direct speech when there is no verb of saying.
> * The message was clear: 'Leave town!'

EXERCISES

Punctuate these sentences by using a colon in the appropriate place.

1 Keats said Beauty is truth, truth beauty.
2 Buy these things at the supermarket soap, toothpaste, washing powder and potatoes.
3 Look at it this way if you cross the amber lights you will probably have an accident.

A semi-colon can join or separate parts of a sentence. When it joins, it can be replaces by a full stop; when it separates, it can be replaced by a comma. Think of it as a weak full stop or a strong comma. Its main uses are:

1   To separate items in a list of long phrases or clauses.
    *   When you go fishing you will need the following: a rod and a reel with fishing line on it; some bait which is suitable for the type of fishing you intend to do; spare hooks, weights and tackle; sandwiches, coffee and spare clothing.

2   To bring together several short sentences on the same topic.
    *   The fire roared; the shadows danced; the wine flowed; the music began.

3   To indicate a slightly longer pause than a comma would suggest.
    *   Try to tackle the more difficult question first; this will probably draw out the best in you.

4   The semi-colon can often take the place of a conjunction or joining phrase.
    *   he could not move; (because) the timber was across his leg.

EXERCISES

◊   Use semi-colons in the following:
1   The dew had settled on the tent the sunshine glistened on the lake a trout jumped in the distance.
2   Sarah didn't want to go to maths yet she liked the subject.
3   After the race his legs became stiff his face lost its colour before long he wished that he had never begun.
4   Looking around the garden there was much to do flowerbeds wanted weeding fruit needed picking vegetables needed digging.

POINTER (:–)

A pointer is not widely used nowadays, but is another symbol employed to introduce examples or lists.

BRACKETS

Using brackets is the clearest way to show that a group of words is interrupting the main flow of meaning, e.g. He thought (so he told me) that he had won.
    *   On the way home from work (what a day!), I saw a nasty accident.
    Note that both these sentences would still make sense without the expressions in brackets.

DASHES

Dashes are used in the same way as brackets, but are preferable because visually they do not break into the sentence so abruptly. They can also be used to indicate a break in sense.

*   Did you know that – excuse me there's someone at the door.

or to show hesitant speech:

*   Well – I didn't know – it has to be said.

Try to avoid using dashes in a sentence where there are hyphens.

*   mother-in-law – God bless her – is coming to stay.

INVERTED COMMAS (speech marks)

These are used in three ways.

1   To show which words are **actually spoken.**

*   'I can only guess,' said my brother, 'where all the people have gone.'

Note

*   only the words spoken have speech marks around them;
*   if the words spoken are a question or exclamation, the ? or ! mark is used **inside** the last of inverted commas
*   you may use double **or** single commas; whichever you decide to use, keep to it; don't change from one style to another. If you have to use inverted commas within direct speech as well as starting and ending it, use a different method of each.

2   To enclose words which are direct quotations, either a passage or single words.

e.g. You have spelt 'where' instead of 'were'.

3   To enclose titles of books, plays, records, names of ships or pubs.

*   The first hymn was 'Praise my soul the King of Heaven'.
*   'Atlantic Challenger' beat the record.
*   Turn right at 'The Poachers'.
*   'Stories of my Time Lake' by John Tristan.

QUESTION MARKS

These are often forgotten about, especially when you are rushing to finish a piece of writing. Always check carefully that you have included a question mark at the end of any sentence which is a question. Remember to put the question mark at the end of the actual words of the question and always put it **inside** the last inverted commas or speech marks.

'How much more can you carry?' she asked.

But

She asked how much more you could carry.

EXCLAMATION MARKS

Use an exclamation mark to show that words are being used very forcefully.

* 'Go for it!' he screamed.

Note that

1 exclamation marks, like question marks, go **inside** the final speech marks;

2 words like 'yelled', 'shouted' etc., which imply that something dramatic is going on, are usually associated with exclamation marks;

3 do not over-use exclamation marks;

4 using question marks and exclamation marks together should be avoided.

THE APOSTROPHE

These have two main uses.

1 To show that a letter has been left out. It is frequently used with pairs of words. Note that in all the given examples the apostrophe is inserted where the missing letter would have been.

Examples:

  do not *becomes* don't
  did not *becomes* didn't
  had not *becomes* hadn't
  is not *becomes* isn't
  it is *becomes* it's
  would not *becomes* wouldn't
  were not *becomes* weren't
  are not *becomes* aren't
  have not *becomes* haven't
  she is *becomes* she's

Remember: if you use an apostrophe with it's, then it is ALWAYS before the 's' i.e. It's.

2 To show possession.

Rule 1 *If the possessor does not end in 's' then add apostrophe 's'.*

* the boy (the boy's tortoise)
* the lady (the lady's shoe)
* the girl (the girl's motorcycle)
* Sheila (Sheila's geraniums)
* John (John's new daughter)

Rule 2 *If the possessor ends in 's' then add an apostrophe.*

* boys (the boys' team – a team of boys)
* girls (the girls' uniform – the uniform of the girls)
* dogs (the dogs' home – the home of the dogs)

Rule 3 *If a person's name ends in 's' then either an apostrophe or an apostrophe plus 's' is added.*

You should add an apostrophe 's' for short names but only the apostrophe for longer words.

* James's football

     *   Antonius' story.

Note

1   that collective nouns such as men, women, crowd, children – words which have changed to form plurals which do not end in 's' – take 's:
 * men's voices
 * women's room
 * children's play area.

2   'its' and 'theirs' have no apostrophe when showing possession:
 * This is its home.

THE HYPHEN

This has four main uses:

1   To join two or more words together to form a compound word, e.g. clear-headed, father-in-law.

2   As a guide to pronunciation, when a prefix ending in a vowel is added to a word beginning with a vowel, e.g. re-employ, co-operative.

3   To avoid confusion in words like re-covered/recovered re-formed/reformed.

4   When a prefix is added to a noun or adjective which begins with a capital letter, e.g. non-English, pro-French.

PUNCTUATION EXERCISES

▷   These sentences are incorrectly punctuated. Punctuate them correctly.

1   john and sue went to basingstoke station on their way to stay with their relatives

2   look out yelled peter the lorry is going to crash

3   as the boy's room, was very untidy I told him off about it;

4   ill find an answer to that one said sheila 'with a smile on her face'.

5   hi you who me yes you what do you think youre doing there jane

▷   The following passage needs 40 punctuation marks to help it make sense. Can you find them?

     jeremy and jane planned to go to cornwall for their summer holidays taking sarah and anne with them will it be okay for us to stay with you jeremy asked his mother in an eager voice of course you can she said id be delighted to see you the village is very quiet id be glad of your company lets hope that the weather is fine said jane later otherwise well all be getting on each others nerves

GRAMMAR

GCSE English will not ask you to explain the finer points of English grammar. Despite this, though, you will certainly lose marks if you ignore some basic rules.

The names of the different kinds of words used in the English language, usually known as the **parts of speech**, are:

1 noun – a word used for naming something.
2 pronoun – a word used in place of a noun.
3 adjective – a word which qualifies or describes a noun.
4 verb – a word which denotes action.
5 adverb – a word which qualifies a verb, adjective or other adverb.
6 preposition – a word which shows in what relation one thing stands to another.
7 Conjunction – a word which connects one part of a sentence with another.
8 Interjection – a word which has no grammatical connection with the sentence.

Here are seven ground rules based on the most common grammatical errors presented in English Language examinations.

1 Do not split infinitives (to go, to run, etc.).
   Examples:
   *   To boldly go, to quickly run. (**wrong**)
        To go boldly, to run quickly. (**right**)
2 Do not end sentences with prepositions.
   *   A preposition is not a word to end a sentence with. (**wrong**)
        A sentence should not be ended with a preposition. (**right**)
3 Take care with 'who' and 'whom.'
   *   Whom owns that bat? (**wrong**)
        Who owns that bat? (**right**)
   *   To who do I give the papers? (**wrong**)
        To whom do I give the papers? (**right**)
4 Beware of sentences such as: Returning home, the farm was silent (**wrong**). This implies that the farm was returning home. Instead it should be: When she returned home the farm was silent (**right**).
5 Nobody, anybody, everyone etc., are all singular words and therefore require singular verbs.
   *   Nobody thought to shout out what they really thought. (**wrong**)
        Nobody thought to shout out what he really thought. (**right**)
6 The -er ending, e.g. better, is used when two things are compared and -est, e.g. best when three things are compared.
   *   He was taller than his sister, but their father was the tallest of the three of them.
7 Neither goes with nor, either goes with or.
   *   Neither one thing nor the other.
        Either Fred or Jim.

SPELLING

Some of the silliest errors can occur in your spelling when you are writing under examination conditions. GCSE, with more emphasis on the work you do during your course, gives an opportunity to keep a watchful eye on this. If you have problems with spelling, the chances are that you will not only lose marks for incorrectly spelled words, but will also tend to fall back on a range of words like 'get' or 'nice'. Remember, however, that most people have words they cannot spell and if you use a dictionary throughout your course then you will be helping yourself to improve.

To get the best out of your dictionary, you need to understand how it is organized.

1 Arrangement: words are generally arranged alphabetically.
2 Head word: the word you will probably be looking for.
3 Different meanings: the most common meaning is given first.
4 Pronunciation: advice will be given on how to say the word.
5 Parts of speech: the dictionary will indicate to which use the word may be put.
6 Types of usage: the word may have a different meaning in different situations.

The English language is notorious for its inconsistencies of spelling, but despite this there are some rules and suggestions which will help you to improve.

PREFIXES

A prefix is a word which goes at the front of another so as to change its meaning.

* anti/climax
* dis/appear

Note:
1 Ante means coming before – ante/natal
2 Anti against or opposite – anti/social
3 Dis or un forms a negative – dis/satisfied
                                   – un/natural
                                   – un/necessary

Remember:
Add the prefix without losing any letters.

SUFFIXES

A suffix is a word tacked on at the end.
Note:
1 Ful – shortened form of 'full' – careful, beautiful, hopeful; only one 'l'.
2 Fully – always add lly – carefully, beautifully, hopefully; two lls.
3 When a suffix is added to a word which ends in 'y', and 'y' is changed to 'i', e.g. beauty – beautiful.
4 When words which end in 'our' have a suffix added, the 'u' is dropped, e.g. vigour, vigorous; humour, humorous.
5 When the suffix begins with the same letter as that which ends the word, that letter is doubled, e.g. keenness, evenness.
6 Some words double the last letter before adding the suffix, e.g. beginning; jeweller; robber.

WORDS ENDING IN 'Y'	1	In the plural of nouns ending in 'y', if the 'y' follows a consonant then it is changed to an 'i' and 'e' is added, e.g. baby, babies; lady, ladies.
	2	When the 'y' comes after a vowel, it is not changed and only 's' is added, e.g. boy, boys; day, days.
	3	The same rules apply to most words ending in 'y' when suffixes are added, e.g. enjoy, enjoyment; play, playful; pretty, prettily; lonely, loneliness.
	4	When adding 'ing' the 'y' at the end of the word is retained, e.g. carrying; copying.

| **VERBS ENDING IN 'Y', 'IE' OR 'YE'** | 1 | When the sound is 'e' (say eee) 'i' comes before 'e' except after 'c', e.g. achieve; believe; but ceiling and receive. |
| | 2 | When the sound is 'a' (say ay) or 'i' (say eye) 'e' comes before 'i', e.g. freight, neighbour, height. |

There are some 'ie' words which do not fit the rules and must be learned individually, e.g. friend; leisure; fierce; weird.

Learn these also:

die, died, dying (tie, tie)
dye, dyed, dyeing
play, played, playing (delay, relay)
pay, paid, paying (lay, say)
try, tried, trying (dry, copy)

NOUN AND VERB CONFUSION	Some words which sound the same have a 'c' for the noun and an 's' for the verb,
	e.g.　practice (noun), practise (verb)
	advice (noun), advise (verb)
	licence (noun), license (verb)

OTHER WORD CONFUSION

Many errors occur in word confusion. Examiners often refer to misuse of the words below in papers they mark. *The sentences show the correct usage.*

1　where/were e.g. I knew where my friends were going.
2　to/two/too e.g. It was too hot for the two of us to go to the beach.
3　there/their/they're e.g. Their bags are over there near the shed where they're (they are) playing.
4　who's/whose e.g. Who's (who is) going to whose house?
5　hear/here e.g. I hear that our neighbours are moving from here.

DICTIONARY

The best aid for spelling is a dictionary; if you don't own one, then it is well worth buying a dictionary to help you with spellings and meanings. When you have looked up a word, make a note of it in a vocabulary book so that you don't need to check it again.

DIFFICULT SPELLINGS

To finish this chapter, here is a list of useful words which often cause difficulty with spelling. See how many of these you can get right.

accelerate	minute
accommodation	humorous
address	manoeuvrable
bicycle	necessary
character	occasion
benefited	possession
development	privilege
committee	occurrence
definite	relevant
embarrass	rhythm
exercise	separate
favourite	sincerely
fortunately	seize
independence	tragedy
interrupt	until

KEY POINTS FOR REVISION

▷ Presentation
      handwriting   ☐YES ☐NO

▷ Expression
          Sentences – three faults   ☐   ☐

          Paragraphs – points to remember   ☐   ☐

▷ Punctuation – Rules and usage
          Capital letter – six uses   ☐   ☐

      Punctuation marks   ☐   ☐

              functions   ☐   ☐

      Full stops   ☐   ☐

              Exercises   ☐   ☐

      Commas   ☐   ☐

              Exercises   ☐   ☐

      Colons and semi-colons   ☐   ☐

              Exercises   ☐   ☐

INDEX